WOMEN AND JOURNALISM

RISJ CHALLENGES

CHALLENGES present findings, analysis and recommendations from Oxford's Reuters Institute for the Study of Journalism. The Institute is dedicated to the rigorous, international comparative study of journalism, in all its forms and on all continents. CHALLENGES muster evidence and research to take forward an important argument, beyond the mere expression of opinions. Each text is carefully reviewed by an editorial committee, drawing where necessary on the advice of leading experts in the relevant fields. CHALLENGES remain, however, the work of authors writing in their individual capacities, not a collective expression of views from the Institute.

EDITORIAL COMMITTEE

The editorial advisers on this CHALLENGE were Steven Barnett and Robert G. Picard

WOMEN AND JOURNALISM

SUZANNE FRANKS

REUTERS
INSTITUTE for the
STUDY of
UNIVERSITY OF
OXFORD JOURNALISM

I.B.TAURIS
LONDON · NEW YORK

Published by I.B.Tauris & Co. Ltd in association with
the Reuters Institute for the Study of Journalism, University of Oxford

Published in 2013 by I.B.Tauris & Co. Ltd
6 Salem Road, London W2 4BU
175 Fifth Avenue, New York NY 10010
www.ibtauris.com

Distributed in the United States and Canada Exclusively by Palgrave Macmillan
175 Fifth Avenue, New York NY 10010

ISBN: 978 1 78076 585 3

A full CIP record for this book is available from the British Library
A full CIP record is available from the Library of Congress

Library of Congress Catalog Card Number: available

Typeset by 4word Ltd, Bristol
Printed and bound by TJ International Ltd, Padstow, Cornwall

Contents

Executive Summary

Journalism is changing, as is the role of women in the workplace, but the two are not always evolving in harmony. Women are better educated and encouraged to achieve at work – just as journalism intensifies, jobs become tougher, and the economic pressures become greater. The digital revolution means journalists can work from anywhere, but what is sometimes viewed as the 'electronic cottage' may also become the 'electronic cage'. As news cycles shorten and demands increase for a 24/7 multi-media presence, so the nature of the work has become more challenging. Meanwhile women still continue to shoulder a disproportionate burden in the home (either because society expects it or they want to) which makes things harder to manage if the workplace becomes more demanding.

Women substantially outnumber men in journalism training and enter the profession in (slightly) greater numbers, but still today relatively few are rising to senior jobs and the pay gap between male and female journalists remains a stubbornly wide one. The same is true across many Western countries. And older women, especially if they have taken a break, find it difficult to retain a place in journalism. The exception to this is in some former Eastern bloc countries where women continue to be well represented amongst the higher echelons of journalism and the media.

The fault line in most Western societies remains the same and this applies across many occupations. What now so often determines whether women are reaching senior posts is whether they have family responsibilities. These exacting roles – such as news reporting or senior editor – which are dependent upon a news or output agenda are difficult for anyone with other responsibilities. The relatively few women who do get these jobs at a higher level have few outside responsibilities; for example, they are far more likely than men to be childless.

Since the late 1980s the drive for female audiences to fulfil advertising targets benefited women journalists who were hired to provide a diet of softer, lifestyle, and feature journalism. And many of the women who did reach the highest levels came from this genre. This has prompted an ongoing debate about the 'feminisation of journalism'.

There are still enduring stereotypes; women predominate on the lifestyle pages, but do not feature much in crime or sport. They are also far less likely to be seen on the front page, which leads to the tendency that 'Men's news is to write on the front page that a fire happened, women's news is to write inside why the guy lit a fire for the third time' (Johnston, 2003). A critical mass of women in journalism at all levels is important in ensuring a greater multiplicity of voices. At the moment, there is a disproportionate lack of female sources, female experts, and even women considered as newsworthy subjects (except when they are victims or royal).

But the digital whirlwind has also created new opportunities and new forms of journalism and this is where women have flourished. They used to leave full-time journalism and write from home as freelancers. Now they can also keep abreast of the news agenda to edit remotely and indeed create whole brands through using social media. And these new ways of consuming media have also enabled women journalists to benefit. Where they can find new ways of doing things and when they carve a new niche, branding themselves in new forms – through a blog or even as a war reporter – this is where women have successfully reinvented themselves. When they enter existing structures they tend to be less successful. There is still evidence of a boys' club and usually where there is a less transparent process, within a corporate hierarchy, then women lose out.

In the traditional structures of journalism there are many junior women but still no clear path of advancement – the same issues recur that have been discussed for over a generation, ever since equal employment rights became a political reality. A number of exceptional individuals have achieved but this has not transformed the culture. There is a tendency to think that the argument has been won, but the concrete evidence shows a stubborn resistance to change across many Western countries – though in the public-service media and in the Nordic countries things are more equal. It may be that in some ways the circle of intense demands and a wish to be involved in family life cannot be squared. Nevertheless, especially because at least a fifth of women today will not have a family, these arguments urgently need to be restated and recast for a new generation and a new digital environment – hence this challenge.

1

Introduction

1.1 Backwards and forwards – onwards and upwards

'Is there any sexual reason why a woman should be a less accomplished journalist than a man? I can find none.' This was the question posed in 1898 by that stalwart feminist writer Arnold Bennett in his publication *Journalism for Women: A Practical Guide*. He had observed the considerable hurdles facing women who wanted to succeed as journalists, as in almost every other workplace at that time. 'A few determined, pioneers . . . found their way into newsrooms but they faced multiple obstacles, notably a lack of educational opportunities, the prevailing view that the woman's place was in the home, and fierce resistance from a largely male workforce' (Lonsdale, 2013). There was a small band of female journalists in the early days of mass media who managed to negotiate a way through, like the remarkable Nellie Bly in the US (Fahs, 2011) or women such as Frances Power Cobbe or Alice Meynell writing in the English press at the turn of the twentieth century (Grey, 2012), the Prussian-born Hulda Friedrichs and the pioneering Swedish journalists Wendela Hebbe and Ester Blenda Nordström. Nevertheless, the participation of women in the journalistic workforce – and certainly in areas beyond strictly feminine topics – was a painfully slow process.

The route of women's entry into the modern workplace altogether has not been a steady and gradual path towards emancipation. There are surprising advances and early examples of success, which were subsequently reversed. The history of women's employment during both world wars demonstrates plenty of cases where what was previously seen as unthinkable suddenly became commonplace – and then once the landscape changed those same opportunities were just as swiftly withdrawn (Summerfield, 1984). Sometimes it is a case of two steps forward followed by one or more steps back. The history of women's entry into journalism is full of such examples.

In the entire twentieth century there were hardly any female editors of UK broadsheet papers. Yet already in 1891 Rachel Beer was editing the *Observer*, one of the most distinguished and venerable newspapers on Fleet Street, and two years later she became editor of the *Sunday Times* (Coren & Negev, 2011). Neither paper has ever employed any female editor since then. Similarly there was a female editor of one of the Northcliffe regional titles in 1939, when Margery Kirk Gatey took over the *Exeter Express and Echo*, but that was the last time until 1990 that any woman rose to such heights in a local paper. The first BBC News service was overseen by Hilda Matheson in 1927. It was not until the next century that a woman would again be running news at the BBC. Similarly the first ever political series launched on the BBC in November 1929, *The Week in Westminster*, was produced by Margery Wace (Franks, 2011).

Here as in later years it was sometimes easier for women to forge a way when things were still novel and in a state of flux, but before established rules and practices had become embedded. In this case it was three years later in 1932 that the BBC, in common with many other employers, moved to introduce an official Marriage Bar (Murphy, 2011) which would inevitably impede women's progress, as they were obliged to resign from the Corporation after their wedding.

According to census figures in 1901, the number of women working as journalists was 1,249, around 9% of the total, and by 1931 that figure had risen further to 3,213, around 17%. Yet thirty years and a world war later in 1961, the proportion of female journalists was barely 20%. The reasons for this lengthy period of stagnation in women's participation in journalism at a time of rising news consumption and expansion of the BBC include the aforementioned introduction of the Marriage Bar and, in other news organisations without a formal Marriage Bar, the convention that a woman journalist would leave work after marriage because the antisocial hours were contrary to the demands of a wife and mother. Moreover, during this period the National Union of Journalists itself pursued discriminatory policies, including suppressing female wages and imposing limits on the number of females accepted onto training schemes.

Even so the profession offered wider access than others. While in the inter-war years women made up over 50% of teachers, and nursing was an exclusively female profession, in 1931 they made up less than 1% of architects and lawyers, 2% of dentists, and about 7% of doctors. In effect then, journalism presented opportunities for educated women, albeit much of it confined to writing about narrow and traditional areas of women's interest (Lonsdale, 2013).

In the second half of the twentieth century there were still multiple examples of outright prejudice hampering women's ambitions in journalism. When the aspiring writer Nora Ephron graduated in the US in 1962, she applied to work on *Newsweek* magazine but was told that women were not allowed to be writers there, so she had to settle for being a mail girl, confined to the post room (Collins, 2012). Some years later there was a famous fightback by the women who worked on *Newsweek,* objecting to the limitations placed upon them (Povich, 2012). But these limitations were hardly an exception. The same attitudes of discrimination against women in journalism could be found across the profession, in print and broadcasting.

Three years after the passing of the first UK gender equality legislation and two years before its final implementation, a confidential BBC report in 1973 revealed a wide range of hostility towards women in the corporation.[1] On the prospect of female newsreaders it quoted a senior manager observing how 'women have class bound voices unsuitable for news reading . . . [and] may introduce emotion'.

On the possibility of hiring women reporters it noted that women would be 'unable to work in the cold and wet . . . and (are) not able to make overnight stays on location with a man as wives would not like it'. Another senior male editor, commenting on the prospect of employing female reporters, said that 'although he had interviewed many women for reporter jobs he had "never found any woman with the remotest chance of working in that capacity" . . . he believes that women are simply not able to do hard news stories . . . [but] "see themselves as experts on women's features"'.

The same editor agreed that he would have liked to recruit women as that would give a spread of knowledge in the newsroom, noting that:

A huge percentage of the audience is female and journalists of their sex are qualified to identify interesting stories on their behalf. When a woman is married her knowledge of the subjects that interest women is thereby increased but of course marriage makes it more difficult for women to work on shift.

In 1964 the first woman news duty editor had been appointed and she subsequently went on to become a duty editor in the Parliamentary Unit in 1970. But the same 1973 report quoted a senior manager in the radio newsroom who explained that 'Young male journalists do not like working in the Parliamentary Unit, where there is a female Duty Editor in charge.' And Jenny Abramsky, who later in the 1970s was the first woman to edit a mainstream news programme when she took over Radio 4's *PM*, encountered directly this same resistance from a male journalist who requested redeployment in reaction to the prospect of a female boss.[2]

Yet there are also ongoing examples where established practices and attitudes can change relatively quickly; one moment they are accepted wisdom, yet within a brief time they appear antediluvian. Views on news reading are a good example of this. A year after the hostility voiced in the 1973 report, the TV producer Angela Holdsworth recalls joining a deputation to the heads of news and current affairs, requesting that women be allowed to read the news:

> We were told very firmly it was out of the question, how could a woman possibly break news of wars, genocide or rail disasters? She wouldn't be taken seriously; people would be looking at her ear-rings or hair-do.[3]

Then a few months later in April 1975 Angela Rippon made her ground-breaking debut on the BBC 1 flagship *Evening News* programme. The Director of Television commented later upon Rippon's debut that: 'Barriers crashed, taboos lay shattered and Lord Reith probably stirred and muttered in his private Valhalla.' And Rippon herself remarked in an interview that 'I knew if I made a hash of it no woman would be allowed another chance for at least 5 years.'[4] Broadcast news, in this respect, has never looked back, which shows that change, when it does come, can be fast and transforming.

However, it is often easier to make such a high-profile symbolic change than to engage with detailed structural problems that are linked with embedded prejudice. Even today, the landscape of women working as journalists in the early twenty-first century remains an uneven one. Whilst some of the ideas still being expressed in the years following the swinging and liberated 1960s now seem outdated, even in a transformed digital environment there remain patterns of gendered employment and attitudes which have proved intractable and immune to change. Take the following snapshots of journalism in the UK over the recent past:

- In 2013 there is only one national daily newspaper in the UK edited by a woman; Dawn Neesom at the *Daily Star*. And in 90 years there has never been a female editor-in-chief (director general) of the BBC or at the head of any other major news broadcasting institutions.

- There has only ever been one instance of a woman editing a daily broadsheet newspaper in the UK, which was fifteen years ago when Rosie Boycott was editor of the *Independent* for three months from January to April 1998.
- Even in an age where papers appear online, authorship of the splash or top stories is significant. A study analysing UK newspaper front pages in 2012 (WIJ, 2012) revealed that the great majority (over three-quarters) of stories featured, and in some papers up to 90%, are written by men.
- Research of by-lines across a range of UK national newspapers in 2011 (Cochrane, 2011) and again in 2012 (Appendix 1) revealed that the overwhelming number of stories in most areas are written by men, so that the average ratio is 78:22, though there were large variations according to subject. In some cases the figures were fairly balanced, but in other areas there were days on end where female by-lines were almost non-existent.
- The newly inaugurated British Press Awards in late 2012 chose nine judges to decide upon the winners. Eight of them were men and the ninth was billed not by any mention of her achievements in the industry, like her fellow judges such as Philip Knightley or Kevin Marsh, but only by her gender as 'Fleet Street's First Female Editor' (*Press Gazette*, 2012a).
- At the well-established UK Press Awards in 2013 the ratio of female to male winners was 4:17 – the lowest it had been in five years.
- When the Inquiry into the Culture, Practices and Ethics of the Press by Lord Justice Leveson in 2012 heard evidence from the great and the good in the world of UK journalism, there were around 200 witnesses who were in some way connected to journalism, but less than one in six of these were women[5] – excluding those witnesses who attended because they were celebrities or other phone-hacking victims, in both of which categories women were well represented.
- A week after the Leveson report appeared and the leading editors were summoned by the Prime Minister in December 2012 to discuss proposals for change, a young journalist Josephine McDermott tweeted: 'BBC News channel shows parade of white, middle-aged male editors arriving at Downing St, bar Sarah Sands. Cd that be problem with press?'

Although these observations are taken from the picture of contemporary UK journalism, most of them also apply to the composition of the media internationally, with a few limited exceptions. Successive surveys of the journalism workforce across most Western nations over the past 15 years show repeatedly that, whilst at entry levels there is a reasonable balance between the genders, at the senior levels there is a preponderance of men. And the higher the age, the wider is the gender pay gap. The ongoing evidence, analysed later in more detail, indicates that there remain today both vertical gender segregation and also horizontal segregation in the way that journalists are employed in the UK, as in many other Western countries. Despite enormous changes there are still places where women have yet to achieve anything like a critical mass and where there is an ongoing cultural bias against them. However, the nature of journalism in a digital 24/7 multimedia environment has also changed and in some cases intensified. There is a much discussed revolution under way in the news industry, which further begs the question of what are the relevant underlying trends for the prospects of female journalists in a more fragmented, globalised, and diverse media landscape?

The roles played by women outside of the home have continued to evolve in the period following the first equality legislation of the 1970s. Issues such as the pay gap or sexual harassment in the workplace are much debated, if not resolved. Yet despite this awareness there are still prevailing expectations about the responsibilities of women within the family and fierce public 'having it all' style arguments which intermittently rage about this topic.[6] It is therefore difficult to disentangle the extent to which better prospects for women in journalism are invariably contingent upon wider societal adjustments, well beyond the scope of this analysis.

Nevertheless, there is an argument that, as journalism and the media play a role in moulding public consciousness, there is a duty upon them to include a wider range of voices at all levels. Sue Matthias, editor of the *Financial Times Weekend Magazine* and former chair of the pressure group Women in Journalism, is clear about this: 'A good and successful newspaper should reflect the society it's reporting on. If women are not in the fabric of the organisation, you've got a worse product' (Janes, 2011). It is this which makes the consideration of women and journalism something which is significant beyond issues of straightforward equity in employment matters. If there is not a wide diversity at all levels producing the output, this may affect the nature of the product; in particular whose voices are being heard and how stories are being told.

1.2 Where does it all begin? The feminisation of journalism education

There has always been ambivalence about the extent to which journalism may be viewed as a profession (Ornebring, 2009) and much debate about the whole construct of professionalism in this context (Aldridge & Evetts, 2003). These considerations have been mirrored by the variety of routes into journalism, which have evolved since the early twentieth century. Historically, the pattern of apprenticeship and indentures, usually through the local or regional press, was the commonest way to embark upon the career ladder. For the lucky few this would develop into shifts and eventually maybe a staff posting on a national paper. There was an attitude of 'school of real life' as a necessary training for successful journalists and a disdaining of higher education as a useful preparation for the workplace. There are still routes into journalism that bypass much formal training and depend upon a serendipity of connections and networks whereby a bright youngster may end up working for the national media. But increasingly these individuals would also have experienced at least some form of higher education.

However, the dominant change in recruitment practice has been the growth in academic journalism training, following the US model, where universities offer specific undergraduate and postgraduate courses as a preparation for the industry. And it is this 'academisation' of the route into journalism which has presented an interesting perspective for women. This is because, ever since these courses originated and started to multiply, they have been increasingly dominated by female participants, though not by female faculty where women remained in the minority: 'being a journalism academic was seen as the prerogative of older men' (Bromley, 2013). This pattern of gradually increasing numbers of female journalism students occurred in the US where academic journalism training first emerged, but it was then replicated in many other countries, including the UK.

Academic journalism training in the US began at the University of Missouri in 1908, when female students made up 15% of the first class. In 1958 one-third of the 2,500 graduates from American journalism courses were women, by 1971 they had become the majority, and in 1984 they already represented 60% (Delano, 2003). Concerns and queries about the implications of this imbalance were already being raised in the 1980s. A study by Maurine Beasley and Kathryn Theus set out to explore 'the ramification of the change from a male majority to a female majority among journalism students nationally', asking whether journalism education was becoming a 'pink collar ghetto' (Beasley & Theus, 1988). Women were plentiful in the student body but the question was raised – what happened next? The evidence revealed that, even though women were taking courses and graduating in significant numbers, they were not as likely to get entry jobs in journalism as male graduates and, even when they did so, this progress was not sustained to take them into the higher ranks. Both an industry-wide study in the US by Dow Jones and a detailed study of successive graduating classes at the University of Maryland confirmed these patterns (Beasley & Theus, 1988: 45). Men with a journalism degree were more likely to find a job in the industry. This was particularly true in the areas of newspapers and broadcasting. Women's chances were somewhat better in local weekly papers and in magazines.

The 1988 research by Beasley and Theus interviewed graduates from previous years and found the same pattern that recurs in much analysis of gender patterns of journalism employment. The women journalism alumni were on average younger and less likely to have children. There was a noticeable pay gap that increased with the age of the cohort, where the men were earning larger salaries and in higher status jobs. Not for the first time the question was being asked why women were graduating in such high numbers but then unable to capitalise upon this training once they reached the workplace? One answer came from an alumna in the study from the 1978 cohort who observed that 'journalism school did a good job with skill-preparation mechanics but it taught no workplace-setting skills. It has the "ivory tower" syndrome' (Beasley & Theus, 1988: 127).

When this same phenomenon was examined more recently, there was a further twist. In a 2005 survey by the American Society of Newspaper Editors the proportion overall of women in newsrooms remained pretty much unchanged at 37%. This was contrasted with the roughly 2:1 proportion in favour of women taking journalism courses at undergraduate and master's levels – so that the numbers were almost exactly reversed between student cohort and those in the professional newsrooms. However, when the figures for women in the early years of a career were disaggregated, it appeared that they outnumbered men at 54% of the total. This was the first time that there had been an imbalance in favour of women, but given the overall figures it was clear that something was subsequently 'driving women from the newsrooms'. And this posed the question: 'Why do some women who study journalism in college, later decide to leave full time newsroom jobs?' (Everbach & Flournoy, 2007).

It is not just in the US that the gradual preponderance of female journalism students has become apparent. A number of studies across the world all demonstrate the same pattern in places as far apart as Australia (Grenby, 2009), Romania (Avadani, 2002), Lebanon (Melki, 2009), and South Africa (Nyondo, 2011). In Germany too there are plenty of female journalism students but far fewer women working in the industry. One analysis attributed this to the 'friendliness trap', where women studying journalism demonstrate good communication skills but are not assertive enough to compete successfully for good jobs (Frohlich & Holtz-Bacha, 2008: 98).

University journalism training had already made a brief appearance in the UK early in the twentieth century. For twenty years from 1919 to 1939 London University ran a small newspaper diploma and in the latter years women began to outnumber men as students on the course. But whereas nearly all the men found jobs, only about half of the women were successful in entering the industry, according to the Newspaper Society representative on the course committee. By the end, the women students outnumbered men in the ratio 33:27, 'suggesting an awareness that, as in America, pre-entry training might compensate for the apprenticeships that were unlikely to be available to women' (Delano, 2003: 275).

Meanwhile there was evidence that, when the Second World War started and 'prejudices were shelved for the duration' across the workforce, quite a number of these graduates were successful in finding work as general reporters, albeit for a limited time (Hunter, 1996).

In the modern period journalism education in the UK began with Cardiff University's postgraduate newspaper course in the 1970s and today there are hundreds of university courses at a range of higher education institutions which include journalism in all varieties – from broadcasting to sport to digital multimedia. As journalism education started to grow, the trends towards an increasingly female student body were the same (Bromley, 2009). By 2012 female students were outnumbering men by at least 2:1 in many of the most well-established journalism programmes. City University, one of the oldest and largest journalism departments in the UK, admitted 369 female students compared to 170 men in 2012. Twenty-five years earlier, in 1987, the recruitment had been slightly in favour of men (57), compared with women (55). Similarly, at Cardiff the total journalism student body in 2012 (undergraduate and postgraduate) was 405 women and 197 men. And in Bournemouth the aggregate enrolments over the past five years showed a 64:36 split towards women.

Women have been studying journalism and graduating from UK journalism departments in substantial numbers for decades, but they are still not well represented at the higher levels of the industry. Commenting on the findings in a 2011 survey which showed how few women were reaching the higher echelons in journalism, Roy Greenslade, the former *Daily Mirror* editor and now a Professor of Journalism, puzzled over this 'disappearance' of female journalism graduates, wondering how the profession could remain so male-dominated when the classes he was teaching were increasingly full of young women (Greenslade, 2011).

In the contemporary workplace an increasing proportion of journalists have come through this route of academic training in a university – up to and including editors of national newspapers and distinguished network broadcasters. Historically though, the evidence has been that women were more likely to follow the route of formal journalism education as a way of becoming journalists because they have fared less well through informal networks. In a fragmented and diverse workplace, journalists still do enter the workplace by other means, but where almost half the population go to university there are now very few who become journalists without some kind of higher education or university experience (Milburn, 2012).

Another way of capturing this trajectory of women as early starters in journalism but failing to win the later prizes is to look at university media in the wider sense. This would argue that, even though a student does not a pursue a specific *course* in journalism, if they aspire to a *career* in journalism they might well seek to publish or contribute to university media or publications, no matter what subject they are taking for a degree. Some of the most distinguished journalists have made their entry into the field through this route, in particular as editors of or contributors to university newspapers.

However, here too there is a similar pattern. When the same Women in Journalism survey about the comparatively small numbers of female by-lines appeared in 2011 (barely 22% over a month of counting), which prompted Roy Greenslade's observations cited above, a parallel survey examined prize-winning student publications by gender by-lines, to find the participation of women in the best student output. The research, titled 'Where do All the Female Journalists Go?' (Cox, 2012), analysed six of the prize-winners of the main student journalism competitions in 2011 and 2012. Once again there was an imbalance between the numbers of women who had succeeded in the world of student journalism and the proportions who were making it in the post-university paid workplace. The by-line count for women writing in the student papers was proportionately over twice as many as that in the survey of national papers. Similarly another survey, by City University, of the editors of the leading student newspapers since 2005[7] also found that a slightly higher proportion were women – a ratio which did not translate into the working world of journalism.

There is the obvious caveat that not everyone who participates in student media or writes for their university newspaper would necessarily want to enter journalism. However, there is no reason why this is more likely to be the case for one gender than the other. So this still begs the question:

> *All the women who are interested in journalism enough that they write for their university newspaper and all the women who apparently take journalism courses, what happens to them? . . . if fairly equal numbers of women and men are actively trying to break into journalism and for some reason the women aren't succeeding, then this needs to be looked at more closely. (Cox, 2012)*

2

Where Are the Women?

The good news is that in many ways youngish women starting out as journalists are not doing too badly at all. In fact this is a trend which extends beyond any career in particular. Girls are showing improved performance at school, gaining better qualifications; they are also outnumbering boys in higher education. As a consequence, the evidence is that, probably for the first time in history, there is a discernible pay gap in favour of women. If one restricts the field to young, well-educated, and childless professionals in their twenties then it is apparent in many areas that young women are doing better than men (Franks, 1999). The same extends to journalism. According to a survey by Mary Ann Sieghart and Georgina Henry which questioned over 500 journalists, already over a decade ago younger women were starting to earn (slightly) more than men (Sieghart & Henry, 1998).

The problem is, what happens next? All the workforce surveys show the same trends across the news industries in Western countries of vertical segregation; women cannot seem to climb to the top in the news industry in any sustained way. There are some isolated examples in the top ranks but they are not followed up. Whilst women may be making a reasonable start, they pretty soon fade away. The higher up the hierarchy, the fewer women and the wider the gender pay gap. This is the evidence produced in the UK by successive Skillset reports, in particular those which focus on the television industry in the UK (Skillset, 2010) and also apparent in the wide-ranging 2002 Journalism Training Forum report *Journalists at Work*. Ten years later the National Council for the Training of Journalists carried out another survey of the UK journalism workforce and the picture was little changed. Women journalists are on average younger than men, whilst male journalists receive a higher average salary than women (£35,000 compared to £27,500).

Further afield the same trends are revealed by the annual American Society of Newspaper Editors surveys (Everbach & Flournoy, 2007) and the Women's Media Foundation 2012 report on the state of women in the US media (Women's Media Center, 2012). In 2011 the International Women's Media Federation published a comparative survey, across 59 countries, which reported a variation of these same trends describing conditions in the US and Western European countries (IWMF, 2011). The same patterns extend across different media platforms. There has been an anecdotal expectation that women should be doing better in online and new media, on the basis that it is less hidebound and might offer possibilities that were not so office-based. But preliminary evidence in the US and from elsewhere shows that the emerging platforms do not make a difference and very few women serve as editors or senior executives of the top online sites (Chambers et al., 2004: 235; Poindexter, 2008: 71; Poynter, 2013a). Another international survey indicated that 36% of online news stories were reported by women and 64% by men (GMMP, 2010).

In Europe, the initial findings from an ongoing EU study on the gender breakdown of media decision-makers across Europe indicate that the results will demonstrate similar patterns.[1] In Western European (but not the Nordic or Eastern European[2]) countries there is a stubborn resistance to female presence at the highest echelons in journalism, as proprietors, owners, or senior managers. Above a certain level, sightings of women are sparse, if they exist at all. In Angela Merkel's Germany, for example, only 2% of newspaper editors are women (Delius, 2012). Similarly, in France there are few women holding senior positions in media organisations and across the profession they are disadvantaged in both pay and job security (IWMF, 2011), although in February 2013 Natalie Nougayrède was appointed as editor of *Le Monde*. And in Australia research by the website New Matilda which analysed the roles of women at senior levels in the media also reveals the same pattern (New Matilda, 2013). As in the UK, only one of the 16 major national papers is run by a woman – Michelle Gunn who edits *The Australian*'s weekend edition. And only 15% of the largest 27 regional Australian papers have women in the editor's chair. But what does emerge from both the Australian and the EU analyses is that women are inclined to do better in public-service media than the commercial and privately owned.

The pay gap between male and female journalists is also a global problem. An International Federation of Journalists study in 2012 compared journalists' salaries in 16 nations across the world, from developed to developing countries (Central European Labour Studies

Institute and Wage Indicator Foundation, 2012). In every case there was a gender pay gap but it showed big variations between areas. Europe had the highest salary levels but also some of the greatest disparities in gender pay. In Belgium the gap between male and female journalists pay was 25%, closely followed by Indonesia at 22%, whereas in some other parts of the world, such as Brazil and Argentina, it was not nearly as wide.

Such is the concern about the lack of senior female journalists in Germany that there were calls in 2012 to establish a 30% quota. The Pro Quote group demanded that over the next five years 30% of the executive jobs in editorial departments across the German media should be filled by women. This follows in the wake of a wider demand for women to be better represented on company boards across Europe, a policy which has been promoted by the German labour minister, Ursula von der Leyen. In 2010 Deutsche Telecom became the first major German company to implement a 30% quota and amongst media groups the financial daily *Handelsblatt* introduced a similar quota the following year. Sandra Maischberger, a prominent TV presenter, supported the demand for a quota: 'A few years ago, I was still completely convinced that it was only a matter of time before the glaring absence of women in the executive class in our industry would be rectified. In some areas – for example, at [public broadcaster] ARD, which is now run by a woman – some things have changed. But there is lot still to be done.'

2.1 Getting older

One of the clearest patterns of women's experience in journalism revealed in the quantitative surveys is that of the age distribution across the profession. What all the analyses show in varying degrees is that the female workforce is on average considerably younger than the average male journalist cohort. This has raised particular concern in television where 55% of women in TV are aged 35 or over compared with 72% of men (Skillset, 2010). *The Times* columnist Caitlin Moran, self-appointed successor to Germaine Greer – and a leading voice of modern feminism, with over 400,000 Twitter followers – has highlighted this disparity in a variety of colourful ways.

Men visibly age every day but women are supposed to stop the decline at around 37, 38 and live out the next 30 or 40 years in some magical bubble . . . so Moira Stewart and Anna Ford got fired when they hit 55, whilst 73 year old Jonathan Dimbleby slowly turns into a f***ing wizard behind his desk . . . the BBC makes finding older newsreaders seem like the Holy Grail. But all they have to do is look through the list of people they've sacked. (Moran, 2011)

Over the past few years the issue of older women disappearing from TV screens has become something of a cause célèbre in the UK. A series of high-profile female news presenters (Moira Stewart, Anna Ford, Selina Scott, Julia Somerville) all assert that they have been pushed aside because of their advancing years. According to the columnist Mariella Frostrup:

Watching the small screen on any given night is enough to convince the most sceptical viewer that euthanasia runs rampant in the medium. No sooner do female presenters hit 50, than they disappear faster than Mugabe's opposition. (Quoted by O'Reilly, 2012)

In 2011 the BBC lost a high-profile court case brought by the presenter of the TV programme *Countryfile*, Miriam O'Reilly, who argued that she had been asked to leave on grounds of age (*Guardian*, 2011). The former director general Mark Thompson admitted in the *Daily Mail* that the BBC had 'got it wrong on older women', especially in iconic roles, and declared that 'things would change' (*Daily Mail*, 2012). Some months later his (brief) successor George Entwistle also uttered some warm words on the subject, in response to the newsreader Fiona Bruce's comments on the uneven way that female on-screen journalists were treated, and he also promised that things would change under his jurisdiction (*Guardian*, 2012a). But within a month Entwistle was gone and it is still difficult to see that anything has happened on this front, despite yet more assurances from incoming senior figures (*Independent*, 2013). Indeed further research in 2013 prompted by the Older Women's Commission revealed the same story, indicating that women made up only 18% of TV presenters aged over 50.[3]

The same age profile amongst journalists is also noticeable in the US. Although there are a handful of very high-profile older women anchors – such as Barbara Walters or Judy Woodruff – there are still difficulties for many women who want to stay in television beyond a certain age. One survey demonstrated that, for every five years that women remained as employees in the organised news business, as opposed to leaving or going freelance, their numbers of the total decrease by about five percentage points (Weaver et al., 2007). As in the UK, the most brutal treatment was in TV news where women were 'let go' once they reached a certain age and where the obsession about physical appearance has long dominated their job prospects (Engstrom & Ferri, 1998; Beasley & Gibbons, 2003). Some of them fought back though and a few gained enormous awards when they succeeded in demonstrating overt discrimination. In one such suit in 1999, Janet Peckinpaugh, a former news anchor in Connecticut, was awarded $8.3 million when she was dropped in favour of a younger model. Another famous case was the Kansas news anchor Christine Craft, who later wrote the memorably titled book *Too Old, Too Ugly and Not Deferential to Men,* with a foreword by Larry King the CNN talk show host (Craft, 1991). The title was based upon a focus group finding which prompted Craft's demotion by the station. At that time in the early 1980s there was apparently only one woman aged over 40 working anywhere in the US as a network affiliate news anchor.

However, it is not only in television where older women are a disappearing breed, but across journalism more widely. As outlined above, successive quantitative studies show that the balance of the age profile of the journalism workforce tilts so that amongst the younger age groups there are more women, but as age increases the balance shifts increasingly towards more men. According to a 2012 survey, 21% of female journalists in the UK are aged 18–29, compared with 10% of male journalists. Correspondingly, 61% of men in journalism are aged 40 and over, compared to 45% of women (NCTJ, 2013). The pressure group Women in Journalism specifically addressed this question in a pilot study *The Lady Vanishes – At 45* (WIJ, 2007) which investigated the experience of older (over 45) female journalists across the industry and asked whether they faced discrimination. A series of interviewees spoke of how they felt squeezed out of the workplace once they reached their forties. In some cases this was because news editors were preferring younger journalists, in others it was because older staff were more expensive and there was a conscious decision to hire cheaper and younger versions. Obviously some of these issues apply equally to older men but the figures show that there are far more of them still working in journalism (amongst older age groups) and there are particular ways in which this process affects women. Even some of the much younger women described how they saw older female colleagues being marginalised and in many of the workplaces there were hardly any women over 45. Other interview research (Williams, 2010) revealed in 2010 that in the world of magazines, especially at the more glamorous end of the monthly market, there is an explicit requirement to 'look the part' and 'identify with the readership', which translates into a workplace where many older women in particular no longer have a place. One magazine journalist who moved on from monthlies described the environment as '90% are young, very fashionable women and the 10% who aren't are the MD, one or two of the financial people and the postroom boy . . . it is a lot about: are you wearing the right clothes? do you fit in?' (Williams, 2010: 178).

2.2 Who does what

Taken as a whole, the female journalism workforce in the UK and other Western countries and across different sectors is substantially younger, more junior, and less well paid, compared to their male equivalents. But the pattern of where women are managing to sustain careers in journalism varies substantially. It is not simply the well-aired issue of vertical segregation – that is, women not reaching higher levels of the profession – but also the more complicated matter of horizontal segregation. As in other workplaces, both skilled and unskilled, women working in journalism have a tendency to cluster in particular areas. There is, for example, evidence to show that in particular areas of journalism, especially magazine publishing (both on- and off-line) and a range of 'softer' lifestyle areas, the so-called 'pink ghettoes' where women are employed in large numbers, they are thriving (Delano, 2003: 274). They have colonised whole areas of the magazine industry, from the glossy monthlies to the high circulation weeklies through a huge range of consumer areas. When women first entered journalism in the late nineteenth century it was predominantly as writers about 'female topics' which they were naturally able to make their own, from needlework to child rearing. But this tendency has been problematic. In one way it has been 'a blessing because it opens doors . . . but it is also a curse because the doors frequently open onto a cul-de-sac' (Wyatt, 2000: 72) where women are trapped due to stereotyping, and in some ways the typecasting still prevails.

The invariable problem with gender clustering is that it tends to mean that women's work, whatever it may be, morphs into something of lesser value (Chambers et al., 2004). There are frequently cited examples of this process, such as the status of doctors in the Soviet Union, when it was a predominantly female profession, or the shift from male clerk in the nineteenth century to the female secretary of the twentieth century and the corresponding loss in status and relative pay. So it is worth examining how the journalistic workforce divides by gender in the twenty-first century, who is doing what and how that affects the perception of certain forms of journalism.

One area where women are perceived to have developed a greater presence over the past couple of decades is in the local and regional press. At the *London Evening Standard* Sarah Sands has been well regarded for turning the paper around into a moderately successful and potentially profitable operation and presiding over a largely female senior management team, although Sands has also expressed concern that 'there could be a drift back to male domination' in journalism (Sabbagh, 2013). The first regional editor, in modern times,[4] was Anita Syvret who edited the *Gloucestershire Echo* for 18 years from 1990, part of the Northcliffe Group. By 2012 in the Northcliffe Group[5] roughly one in four of the editors was female. However, upon closer inspection, it appears that it is only on weekly local papers that women have started to make these noticeable gains. As the regional press has gone through tumultuous times and many publications have reduced from daily to weekly, there are still far fewer women in senior positions at daily regional papers. Michelle Lalor has been editing the *Grimsby Evening Telegraph* for over a decade, but she is one of a handful of female editors of daily local papers/websites and interestingly, like Sarah Sands, she has a largely female senior team. The vast majority of the women who have reached more senior positions have done so on weekly papers and their associated websites. The same is true elsewhere; for example, a third of the local papers in Australia are edited by women, but these are predominantly small community and rural outlets (New Matilda, 2013).

There has also been an assumption in the literature that local radio, because of its comparatively lower profile and status in the overall hierarchy of journalism (as with local weekly papers), would be a workplace with a comparatively higher female cohort (Zoonen, 1994). This was certainly not the case in the very early years when Sandra Chalmers (who later edited *Women's Hour*) became the first ever female manager of a local radio station. She was appointed to run Radio Stoke in 1976 and recalls considerable hostility and isolation.[6] However, in the subsequent period of rapid expansion of local radio stations it did appear to become a more welcoming workplace for women (Sebba, 1994), though this does not seem to have been a uniform progression and there are still pockets, unexpectedly, in which local radio is far from an egalitarian environment. In 2012 there was an angry blog from a departing local radio news journalist who highlighted the absence of a solo female news presenter on any one of the 40 BBC Local Radio Breakfast slots (typically the early morning news shows have the largest audiences). In an open letter to George Entwistle (the briefly incumbent BBC DG) Ruth Dixon complained about the 'travesty that female presenters are being discriminated against in local radio' (Dixon, 2012).

This sidelining of women in regional radio presenting has also become an issue in the US. According to research published by the Women's Media Center, out of the 2011 'Heavy Hundred' top radio talk shows across America, only 13 had solo female presenters plus a further three featured women co-hosting with men (Women's Media Center, 2012). So the automatic association of a large female presence with a lower status workplace is not quite so straightforward. However, there is no doubt that highly competitive areas of national media continue to have an uneven record of female employment.

2.3 National by-lines

The mainstream national press is considered amongst the most 'prestigious' areas of journalism which is why a by-line count here is a useful way of gaining some insight into the gender balance in such a high-profile part of the industry. Although by-lines are a fairly crude tool and could be complemented by an analysis of how many individual words are written rather than whole articles, this does give at least an overview of who is being published.

In June 2011 Women in Journalism published a four-week study across seven national newspapers. The results were as shown in Figure 2.1. The average across all seven papers for the four-week period was 78% male and 22% female by-lines.

In 2012 this was followed up by a survey of front-page by-lines (see Figure 2.2). Once again, as in the 2011 by-line survey, the gender breakdown for the front-page stories across the nine papers was 78:22, although there was a wide variation between different publications – from the *Daily Express* which had an equal number of front-page stories written

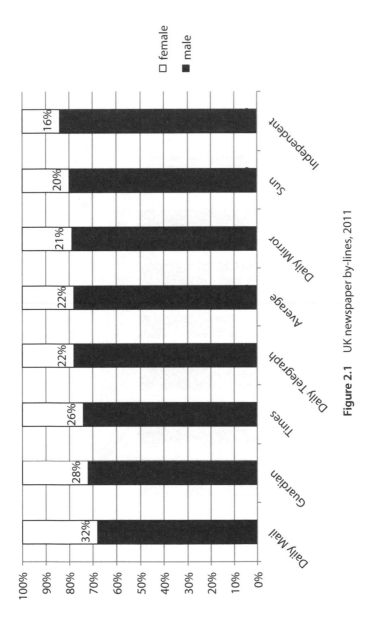

Figure 2.1 UK newspaper by-lines, 2011

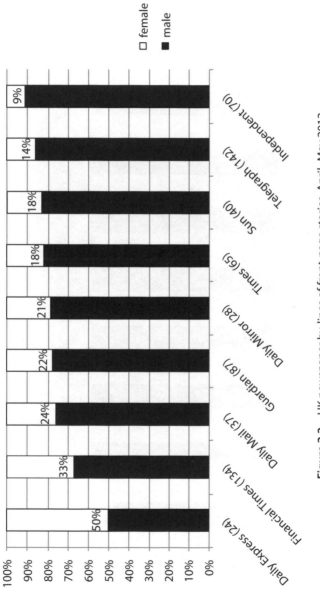

Figure 2.2 UK newspaper by-lines of front-page stories, April–May 2012

female
male

Daily Express (24)
Financial Times (134)
Daily Mail (37)
Guardian (87)
Daily Mirror (28)
Times (65)
Sun (40)
Telegraph (142)
Independent (70)

50%
33%
24%
22%
21%
18%
18%
14%
9%

100%
90%
80%
70%
60%
50%
40%
30%
20%
10%
0%

by women, to the *Independent* where male by-lines outnumbered female by almost 10:1.[7]

There was a further content analysis which, instead of *all* the front-page stories, examined only each day's lead story or splash, and in the case of joint by-lines the first name only was counted. Here the overall result was slightly different – as according to these criteria women only made up only 19% of the total. This 2012 survey also did a gender analysis on the content of the front-page stories, which is discussed further in Chapter 4.

2.4 Newshounds and features bunnies

In autumn 2012 another gender analysis of by-lines was conducted at City University London and this time there was also coding of the different sections of the papers (see Appendix 1). This survey looked at five national papers over seven days, rather than six as in the previous surveys, during two separate weeks, a month apart. The total figures were not dissimilar from the WIJ surveys – but what was of interest was the breakdown which showed a huge variation between subject areas. In some cases, especially but not exclusively the softer lifestyle areas, there were reasonable representations of women, but in other places the number of by-lines was scarce to non-existent. This wide difference in gender by-lines by subject demonstrates what is apparent from interviewing and anecdotal evidence. Women in news organisations at different levels frequently talk of how they are encouraged to do the softer feature lifestyle stories and discouraged from the harder end of news. Here is an example:

> *Working at a regional level, the editors seemed determined to steer me away from 'serious' specialties such as politics or crime and instead hand me fluffy features or celebrity gossip to do. Many hard news story ideas I came up with were handed to a male reporter to deal with instead – despite the ones I completed 'under the radar', so to speak, usually making a strong up-front lead. This sexist attitude – and having little to no interest in writing about fashion – is the reason I left. (Newman, 2013)*

This pattern of clustering was examined in detail by a study in 2010 (Williams, 2010). The only group of journalists who did not recognise

23

it were those on weekly regional papers where the small scale of the operation meant that there was no noticeable gender division of tasks – it was a matter of all hands to the pump. As mentioned above, this is a sector where there are now a significant number of women in senior positions. Aside from weekly regional media there was a general recognition in every other interview that women were far more evident in feature and lifestyle areas. The clustering was noticeable both between organisations and also within them, where women tend to work in certain departments and on certain subject areas.

The underlying motivation for gender clustering is the significant issue here. Using a series of in-depth interviews with women across the journalistic spectrum Williams identifies three possibilities. Some women feel that they have made a positive choice and prefer the lifestyle/magazine/features route because they have a genuine interest in those areas. Indeed, many of the women she spoke to who were working on women's magazines felt empowered by their clustering. One senior magazine journalist said that 'Women's magazines are a way to show that we [women] can do what the hell we want. There are so many women all together doing what we love and do best . . . We've chosen to do it and that's a good thing.' Williams's view (Williams, 2010: 233) is that these women perceive themselves as making a choice in a meritocratic, equal workplace.

A second group of women also spoke of having made a choice to work in features areas. However, their decision was prompted by the working culture – they perceived features as a place with a more palatable and predictable lifestyle. And a third group felt that they had been pressured by external forces into certain areas of work, whereas their preference would have been towards a harder news role. A senior reporter on a mid-market newspaper remarked:

> It is quite normal for there to be a political story to come in and they send a man even though I am standing right there (and have expertise in politics). If it was a very boring press release about some sort of childcare thing, I'll be given it. If I see all the stories on the newsdesk, I can tell you which story I would get.

A senior reporter on a broadsheet observed: 'When I was at Westminster, when there was a ridiculous story about Tony Blair's hair or about the

By Jeremy Gerlis

Tory MPs wearing woolly jumpers, then I'd be sent to do those soft pieces' (Williams, 2010: 240).

Another broadsheet journalist was clear that in such cases it is a problem of basic gender stereotyping which leads to this segregation. 'What they say is that you are either a "newshound" or a "soft features bunny". And yes of course there are more women in features. But you are stuck with that stereotype really. It's hard for a woman to . . . convince them that you should be seen as a "newshound". Even the descriptors 'hard news' and 'soft features' have a gender dimension. It is apparent both from the figures in Appendix 1 and from interviews that political coverage is a particular area (although not the only one) where women's contributions are still very limited. Historically women rarely became political reporters. And just as politics itself was seen as a man's game with very few female participants, so the reporting of politics was centred around a male club. In 1890, the Serjeant at Arms turned down a request by the *Women's Penny Paper* to have a female parliamentary reporter in the gallery, warning darkly that 'the consequences were too difficult to conceive'. Women were finally accepted as members of the Westminster Lobby in 1945 with the appointment of Eirene Jones, later Baroness White, as political correspondent for the *Manchester Evening News*, but they continued to be a rarely sighted species.

In the early 1980s there were only two women members of the Lobby, Elinor Goodman (*Channel 4 News*) and Julia Langdon (*Daily Mirror*), but they were viewed as exceptional. Indeed, Goodman tells a story that she was speaking to an MP in the Member's Lobby once and he referred to a conversation he seemed to think they had had the previous day. She then realised that he had confused her with the only other woman (Langdon) – on the basis that they were perceived as interchangeable representatives of their gender.

Kate Ironside was taken on as a young political reporter for the *Daily Express* in 1988 and found it a tough experience. The *Express* newsroom was almost entirely male and she recalls 'an aggressive, bullying culture'.[8] Meanwhile the male journalists of the Westminster Lobby treated her as a strange and odd breed. She had no doubt that the editor, Nick Lloyd, appointed her as the paper's number three political correspondent because she had good shorthand and as a pretty young thing would appeal to the MPs.

The number of female political reporters has increased since the 1980s, but there are not as many as conventional wisdom seems to think.

When the *Press Gazette* listed the 50 leading political reporters in 2012 they included only three women, ranked at numbers 16 (chief political reporter of the *Financial Times*), 36, and 39 respectively (*Press Gazette*, 2012d). And according to Appendix 1, on some papers – *Daily Mail* and the *Independent* – the imbalance in political reporting in late 2012 is pretty conclusive, with the overwhelming number of stories about politics being reported by men. Neither paper has a single woman on its political team. Overall, the number of women in the Parliamentary Lobby is 23% – almost exactly the same as the proportion of female MPs. But there is only one female political journalist listed in the magazines and periodicals section and none of the daily papers, broadcasters, or the main political websites has a female political editor, so once again, even though there are some women, they are not finding their way to the higher strata in significant numbers. Pippa Crear, political correspondent with the *London Evening Standard,* considers the culture of women in political journalism has become even *less* welcoming during her time in the Lobby. When she first arrived there were twice as many female political editors (Veeneman, 2013).

At the start of 2013 there was a sudden focus on the female deficit in political reporting at the New Year prime-ministerial press conference. David Cameron and Nick Clegg appeared in Downing Street before the assembled mass of political reporters and did not take a single question from a woman journalist. This lacuna started a buzz on Twitter, eventually featuring on Sky TV and in the press. No. 10 issued a defensive response, that there were no women political editors present in the room, so they could not be at fault. Even the political blogger Guido Fawkes remarked upon this gap and felt moved to point out how relentlessly male the Lobby remains (Media Guido, 2013), in yet another article with the title 'Where have All the Women Gone?' He highlighted the eight-man political reporting team of the *Mirror* and the two-man team from the *New Statesman* in particular, both of them perceived as organs of the more progressive end of the spectrum. Yet they are not the only ones and indeed Fawkes himself (aka Paul Staines) has no female journalists – as the blog comments were quick to point out.

The limited role of women in the reporting of politics is also noticeable in the US. In 1988 Joan Snyder, a respected CBS field producer gave a lecture at Berkeley titled 'The Only Girl on the Road' (Beasley & Gibbons, 2003), which was a reference to the famous 1972 account of covering the presidential campaign, *The Boys on the Bus* (Crouse, 1973).

27

However, by 2012 not that much had really changed. A study on the coverage of the presidential campaign showed that three-quarters of the reporting had been by men (4th Estate, 2012). And the very high-profile presidential debates also had an interesting gender dimension. This was only the second time since the debates had begun in 1960 that a female journalist was invited to act as a moderator, the previous occasion having been in 1992. Candy Crowley of CNN anchored the second (of three) Obama/Romney debates on 16 October 2012.

However, the reaction to Crowley's appearance on Twitter and other social and mainstream media afterwards was extraordinary. There was an onslaught of comments and attacks on her appearance and in particular body weight, quite out of proportion to the reaction provoked by any male presenter (Huffington Post, 2012). This was still a role where it did not feel 'normal' to see a woman.

Election coverage in the UK has a similar feel. Joanna Coles (now editor-in-chief of US *Cosmopolitan*) recalls covering the UK General Election as a political reporter in 1997 being 'like a minor stag party'. She remembers how 'leering over pornography, cans of lager and sniggering at women' (Gill, 2007) were a regular part of the behaviour on the campaign bus. The style of how politics is reported – an adversarial, national sport – may be a reason why women have not become more incorporated into this model. And it is a style of coverage focused around the Westminster village which has changed very little. For years it has been a cosy lobby-bound activity where many women feel they are still outsiders (Veeneman, 2013).

After politics, a second area where female by-lines are pretty much invisible (see Appendix 1) is in sports journalism. In some ways this is not so surprising because sport, even more than politics, is perceived as an overwhelmingly male activity. According to a report by the Women's Sport and Fitness Foundation, outside major sporting festivals such as the Olympics, only 5% of media attention devoted to sport in the UK focuses upon women's sporting activity (*Guardian*, 2012b). And a study into sponsorship in the UK calculated that women's sport receives between 0.5 and 1% of the total commercial spend on sport.

Given that most media coverage is of sport which is being played by men, there is still a stark disproportion in who is doing the reporting about it. In 2011 a wide-ranging German survey on press coverage of sport across 80 newspapers in 22 countries revealed that only 8% of the articles were by women (ISPS, 2011): see Appendix 2. And in the UK in 2012 only two of the *Press Gazette* Top 50 Sports Reporters were women (*Press Gazette*, 2012b), although in March 2013 Alison Kervin was appointed by the *Mail on Sunday* as the first ever female sports editor on a national newspaper.

The Olympics of 2012 were seen as a triumph for female sporting achievement and encouraged a perception, because of a few high-profile TV presenters, that there is plenty of female sports reporting – but soon afterwards it appeared as if normal service had resumed. Even the satirical journal *Private Eye*, not widely seen as a champion of women's causes, was moved to point to this imbalance in December 2012. It highlighted the hypocrisy of a *Daily Mirror* editorial which commented that the 2012 BBC Sports Personality shortlist 'avoided last year's embarrassing men only affair' – in 2011 the contest had not featured a single woman (*Private Eye*, 2012). Yet apparently the Sports section of that same edition of the *Mirror* had featured 27 by-lined articles, every one of which was written by a man; it also noted that the only woman pictured on the *Mirror* Sports pages was the girlfriend of Formula One driver Lewis Hamilton.

The gender division by subject areas is not always so predictable. Some parts of the news agenda do have a surprising number of women, despite cultural assumptions. As the figures in Appendix 1 indicate, business and financial reporting is an area which has a surprisingly balanced gender divide, even though this might historically have been considered a man's world. It is particularly evident at the personal finance end of the spectrum, but also in many other areas of financial reporting. And the *Financial Times* in particular, according to the Women in Journalism Front Page survey (see Figure 2.2) had the second highest number of female by-lines and in 2011 employed more female journalists than any other UK national paper. Several senior women on the *Financial Times* spoke of, how under the present management and in particular the editorship of Lionel Barber, it has become a particularly encouraging place for women to work. It may also be a coincidence but Pearsons, which owns the *Financial Times*, was the first major UK company to appoint a female chief executive, Dame Marjorie Scardino (a former journalist), who served as CEO from 1997 to 2012.

Another unexpected area where a range of women journalists have found a voice in recent years is in war and conflict reporting. Historically, this again was very much a male domain, for obvious reasons, with a few rare exceptions such as the legendary Martha Gellhorn or Clare Hollingworth. However, over the past 20 years, a steadily growing number of women of many nationalities and across different media have become celebrated in this area. In the Balkan wars of the 1990s and throughout the fighting in the Middle East and Afghanistan over recent years, there have been notable and prize-winning contributions by female reporters, some of whom faced extraordinary risks.

In 2012 after CNN reporter Lara Logan was attacked and sexually assaulted in Cairo's Tahrir Square, the International News Safety Institute published *No Woman's Land: On the Frontlines with Female Reporters* (INSI, 2012), a collection highlighting the contribution of female war reporters. There is some evidence from this and other accounts, including the despatches and memoirs from many well-known female war correspondents such as the late Marie Colvin, Janine di Giovanni, or Alex Crawford, the Sky News reporter who was the first Western journalist into Tripoli following the overthrow of Gaddafi, that they have evolved a different way of telling the story (Colvin, 2012).

There is a focus upon the human cost of war, rather than weapons and fighting. In this way women have managed to occupy a new and distinctive journalistic space, rather than duplicating or trying to carve up the existing one (Prentoulis et al., 2005). And in many ways women have capitalised upon their differences in order to bring a wider dimension to the reporting. Alex Crawford, for example, speaks of how she is able to access voices, such as the stories of Arab or Muslim women, in a way that would not be possible for a male journalist. Paula Slier is a South African journalist who has a long experience in reporting from the Middle East and she too has pointed to the extra dimensions which women can bring to conflict reporting (Slier, 2013). The BBC's Lyse Doucet describes how Western female reporters become in many situations (INSI, 2012) a type of 'third gender' who can operate outside established norms, a view echoed in the *Daily Telegraph* by Phoebe Greenwood.

In the Israel–Gaza conflict in November 2012, Greenwood observed that the majority of the correspondents reporting on the ground, representing media from all over the world, were women, including a heavily pregnant photographer, Eman Mohammed Darkhalil (Barnett, 2012). But then women are very much part of modern warfare; as the doyenne of modern female war reporting, the BBC's Kate Adie, pointed out already many years ago, contemporary conflict is about civilians.

I have never been in a single riot or war or any other dangerous situation where half the people present weren't female. Who was providing the food, clearing up, looking after the victims, consoling the relatives? It's always women. Usually it's men who are the only people with power . . . the army, police – the ones with guns.[9]

In fact partly in the wake of Kate Adie who became a poster girl of conflict reporting, the ubiquity of the female TV war reporter has even prompted snide remarks, usually from long-standing male correspondents. They have claimed that there is now a 'pretty girl in a flak jacket' syndrome, where attractive young women are specifically sent by TV newsrooms to cover wars, as this juxtaposition entices audiences (Sebba, 1994: 277).

A third significant area where there is a noticeable gender imbalance is in opinion writing. Just as the obituary columns give an impression of a world which has far more than 50% of one gender, the same is true in the comment columns. This pattern is demonstrated in the same two-week content analysis from autumn 2012, see Appendix 3. The *Guardian* datablog, from analysing three national papers and associated websites, found that women had written 26% of the opinion pieces (*Guardian* datablog, 2012).

In the US such is the dearth of female opinion writing that a pressure group and website, the Op-Ed Project, was set up to highlight this issue: www.theopedproject.org. Their figures claim that only 20% of comment pieces in the US media are by women and they campaign for a greater range of voices so that the proportion of women eventually reaches a tipping point. The *Columbia Journalism Review* published a lengthy analysis of this deficit: 'It's 2012 Already: Why is Opinion Writing Still Mostly Male?' (CJR, 2012). They compared the legacy and new media, and found that women had a better chance of publication in digital form (33% compared to 20% in print) but there was a sting. The online comment by women on sites such as the Huffington Post was twice as likely to focus on 'pink topics' described as the four Fs (family, food, furniture, and fashion), plus of course women and gender. In contrast, only 14% of women's op-ed comments in legacy media were on these topics. They attributed this to the silo tendency of new media, where writers speak to like-minded individuals. And the *CJR* emphasises the ongoing importance of comment in the traditional press in agenda setting for the wider media landscape.

Sue Horton, comment editor of the *Los Angeles Times*, expressed frustration with the overwhelming number of men who solicit comment slots compared to women, an estimated 9:1 according to the *Washington*

31

Post. She noticed also that 'submissions from women are more likely to be from writers who are particularly informed, while a much greater share of submissions from men are "dinner party op-eds" – pieces written because the author has an opinion on the subject, not because of any particular standing or expertise.'

In the UK, Caroline Daniel noticed the same reluctance when she was comment editor at the *Financial Times*. Even when they were asked to contribute, women were more inclined to refuse on the basis that they were insufficiently knowledgeable to give a view.

> *When I ran the FT's opinion pages there was a surprising meekness, or even self-censorship among women: few were willing to put their heads above the parapet to advocate an idea. Every day we received up to 50 unsolicited op-ed articles. Only 5–10% came from women. I once asked a senior female business leader to write. Despite decades of experience, she told me she wasn't 'ready to write anything.' (Press Gazette, 2012b)*

Founding editor of the *Independent* Andreas Whittam Smith discussed women and leader writing with Ginny Dougary in a classic book about female journalism *The Executive Tart and Other Myths* (Dougary, 1994): 'Leader writing may be slightly foreign to the temperament of women . . . they don't think it is very clever to set down an opinion . . . the form may be repugnant in some way to women.' Obviously there are some high-profile female columnists who are champions at setting down an opinion, but the overall figures do seem to suggest a lack of gender balance in this area

---

Despite the hurdles faced by many women entering journalism there have been a small number of international superstars who have gained a worldwide reputation for their international and political reporting over the past 50 years. Notable amongst these have been reporters such as Oriana Fallaci from Italy, who became well known as a formidable interviewer, or Christine Amanpour the CNN foreign correspondent, who became a worldwide figure after her reports during the first Gulf War. Two outstanding women who paid with their life for their devotion to pursuing difficult stories were the Irish crime reporter Veronica Guerin and the Russian investigative journalist Anna Politkovskaya.

---

and this even extends to the arts pages.[10] The problem appears twofold. Women are not being asked, but even when they do get approached, they are reluctant to contribute. This links to the lack of female voices in the news, as experts and sources, which is discussed further in Chapter 4.

2.5 Just call me a man

This differentiation of the areas where male and female journalists predominate points to a number of conclusions. Overall it appears that the closer to the harder edge of news reporting and opinion writing, the fewer women prevail – just as the higher up the hierarchy and the age profile then the fewer women and the less they earn in comparison with men. This was revealed in the Sieghart/Henry report, but has since been confirmed by many other surveys, such as the industry-wide Journalism Training Forum survey in 2002 or the Skillset survey into careers in television in 2012. Overall, the 'research shows that the business of organised journalism is a man's world', concluded Massey and Elmore in a 2011 study (Massey & Elmore, 2011) which looked at why so many women were leaving journalism, although it is journalism in particular sectors (see previous section) which women still find it hard to enter in substantial numbers.

Evidence to the Leveson Inquiry in 2012 made clear that the newsrooms of national tabloid papers remain tough workplaces and some women in particular have experienced harassment and bullying. Michelle Stanistreet, appointed in 2012 as the first woman general secretary of the NUJ, believes that 'sexism runs through the entire industry'[11] and that tabloid newsrooms, where she once worked, are 'very hard bitten environments', a position made worse by 'casualisation and insecurity', which was highlighted in a 2012 NUJ survey of female members (NUJ, 2012).

The distinctly individualistic occupational culture of journalism, which often pits individuals against each other (Williams, 2010), also produces a tendency for secretive and less than transparent remuneration. There is a wider literature which shows that women are particularly poor at negotiating individual pay deals and undersell themselves in these situations. In journalism women have therefore lost out on pay rises and a number of those who eventually proved such allegations have won considerable awards. One of the most high-profile examples in recent years was the *Racing Post* editor Fleur Cushman who proved that she was being paid £8,000 a year less by Trinity Mirror than the equivalent man in 2008, and in addition to a pay rise she also received £26,000 in back pay. *Channel 4 News* presenter Cathy Newman describes a similar experience when she worked on the *Financial Times*. Finding that a male colleague on a lower ranked job was being paid £10,000 more, she challenged the management. The response was that she did not have a mortgage and family, so had less need of the money – but she got her rise in the end (Newman, 2013).

At the crudest end there are still cases today where female journalists face versions of outright prejudice. Bethany Usher is a former tabloid crime reporter who broke many important stories – but she recalls how there was a continual undercurrent from her male peers that she ought really to be elsewhere, doing the celebrity news. One woman still working in a senior position on a national tabloid news desk spoke about the hostile attitudes she had faced, including outright sexual innuendo on a daily basis. The news editor of the paper (who was subsequently removed) had repeatedly insinuated that women were not suited to hard news and she should move to features 'where the girls belonged'. She loved the cut and thrust of news and was determined to stay, but that meant she has had to endure considerable harassment and unpleasantness. And the fact that there were not many other women on the news desk did not help.

Other interviews revealed how the best way to survive on a news desk was to become 'an honorary man'. One woman who became a successful regional news reporter (and later a national news reporter), breaking many important stories, recalls that some years ago she worked for a news editor, at a well-known regional paper, who could not accept the idea of a woman in this role. 'He felt comfortable with men and gave them all the best jobs, believing that women (like his own wife) belonged at home and certainly should not be reporting crime and politics.' When she proved herself as a competent and energetic news journalist and he eventually started to trust her with important stories, his reaction was to rename her as 'Bert', 'as his way of accepting a woman could also be a tough minded news reporter'. This interviewee, like many others, was a thrusting news reporter in her twenties but then moved out of news and eventually out of full-time staff employment in her thirties, although she still works as a freelance writer on a national paper.

This is a familiar pattern, that plenty of women start out in journalism but then divert. The next chapter looks in more detail at why it is that women beyond a certain stage are leaving full-time employment in journalism.

3

Beyond the Glass Ceiling

3.1 Highlighting exceptions – the glass menagerie

Many of the reports about women working in journalism use the familiar image of a 'glass ceiling' and query to what extent this exists as an impediment to advancement. But in the diversified and digital workforce of contemporary journalism, evidence shows that a simple glass ceiling is no longer an adequate metaphor. The position is rather more subtle and complicated than can be captured by a single image. If there is a ceiling, then it is more difficult to identify. As Caitlin Moran writes: 'It's difficult to see the glass ceiling because it's made of glass. Virtually invisible.'

Sometimes the ceiling morphs into what Stella Creasy MP, addressing a 2012 Women in Journalism event, referred to as 'the glass menagerie' or the Mrs Thatcher factor, whereby a few women have broken into spheres of influence, which is then cited as evidence that the problem is solved:

> *I think we've come 20% of the way towards a more equal society and then we've hit a buffer where people think 'that's enough now'. We've got some women in Parliament, some women in journalism, some women presenters. Rather than being a glass ceiling, it's become a glass menagerie, where you go, 'hey, there are some women on boards', but it's the same women being circulated. (London Evening Standard, 2012)*

A handful of individuals have achieved something which prompts endless attention and repeated focus and the assumption is that because a barrier has been breached (even if only once) then the situation is permanently resolved. The same pattern can be identified in many different workplaces, according to Creasy. So for example there is no longer judged to be a problem for women advancing in politics because there has already been a female prime minister; or one woman has reached the Supreme Court, so that means gender equality has henceforth been solved in the legal profession. Yet the achievement of a few exceptional individuals does not mean that the landscape for women's advancement has been transformed. Very often this is only the beginning of the solution and if effort is not continually applied then in the longer term very little will change and there will be a reversion towards the default position.

In politics there are fewer women holding very senior positions now than there were just a few years ago. In 1994 there were three national UK papers edited by women and the 'time will tell' school of thought may have regarded that as the start of a steady trajectory. A top News International figure said in 1994 that, on this basis, 'there should be ten women editors by the year 2000' (Dougary, 1994: 96). He was well off the mark, and in 2013 there are only two female editors, Dawn Neesom and Lisa Markwell. There is a wider failure to understand that a few isolated breakthroughs by themselves do not mean that the issue of women's advancement in journalism can be ticked off as a problem solved.

In 2012 the number of women chief executives of FTSE 100 companies halved from four to two. There were also fewer female permanent secretaries at the top of the UK Civil Service than just a few years earlier. The Democratic Audit of the United Kingdom published in 2012 had a long section devoted to the role of women in public life across the spectrum from the judiciary, political representation, public bodies, etc. (Democratic Audit, 2012). While the conclusions noted that there had been some limited improvements in the promotion of greater gender equality, it concluded that 'the UK had a long way to go'. But in particular the report identified how: 'In most areas, the modest initial progress that has been made in improving the representation of women since our last Audit has clearly stalled.'

There was considerable debate in 2012 about the number of women at senior levels in the Civil Service. In the previous five years under the cabinet secretary Lord O'Donnell the number of women appointed to permanent secretary grew to almost 50% across Whitehall, but from 2011 onwards there was concern that the senior civil service was again becoming 'paler and maler'. Jill Rutter, from the Institute of Government, blogged about these shifts and questioned whether the gains women had made under O'Donnell's regime were now being undone (Rutter, 2012), making the same arguments that unless there is ongoing attention towards achieving a more balanced workforce, progress can easily be reversed. In 2012 four female permanent secretaries moved on and no new women were promoted. And it is not as if women are waiting in the wings; none of the ten second permanent secretaries in Whitehall is a woman (Rutter, 2013).

Karren Brady, the first chief executive of a Premier League football team, in her book *Strong Woman: An Honest Account of How to Get to the Top in a Man's World*, emphasised how important it is that women who do achieve hold the door open wide behind them. It is only this way that a critical mass will be reached, instead of a series of individual 'just look at her' style exceptions.

The Fawcett Society has campaigned relentlessly on women's equality issues and Dr Katherine Rake, the former director, is clear why women's advances only seem to reach a given point. 'The number of women at the top often hovers around a third, and then stalls . . . Once women reach that level of visibility,' she suspected, 'there is a feeling they were everywhere, and their presence was becoming a bit too dominant' (Cochrane, 2011). 30% is a relevant figure because a number of institutions, private and public, have taken that as a target for the recruitment of senior women. The BBC, for example, set 30% as its target for senior executives.

Jana Bennett is one of the women who reached the highest levels in the British media. In December 2012 she was given a 'contribution to the medium' award by WFTV (Women in Film and Television) for her career in the BBC, where she arrived as a news trainee in 1978 and eventually became Director of Vision and later President of BBC Worldwide. She reflected upon her experience as a pioneering woman: 'You have to keep taking these steps forward and no organisation should think it is there yet. Why should there be a 30% target for boards if women are half the population? Organisations should be mindful that their investment doesn't walk out the door'. She doesn't believe in quotas but does believe in targets, adding: 'Other countries are ahead of the UK. I think there's a bamboo ceiling rather than a glass ceiling: it stretches but doesn't really break' (Broadcast, 2012).

Looking back upon her time at the top of the corporation, Bennett still senses that there was a way in which her fellow (male) directors, however politely, regarded her as an exception and she was aware that the accepted 'default' position was not one which included a critical mass of women at the top, because, however subtle, it still felt like a 'boys club'. And in particular she noticed that, when things happened via the informal 'tap on the shoulder' routine rather than transparent, merit-based processes, it was invariably men who were appointed and selected for preferment, because that was what felt 'normal'.[1]

Margaret Gallagher, who has written extensively about enduring gender inequity in journalism and in the hierarchy of news (Gallagher, 2001), quotes a Canadian journalist who identified this syndrome, where a few particular individuals are able to succeed rather than there being a shift in the wider culture, as 'One woman at a time . . . One at a time. We barely manage to fill the shoes left by one another.'

3.2 Changing directions . . . sliding glass doors

Young women are entering journalism but at a certain point they are disappearing. The female journalism workforce is proportionately younger. But there is another very obvious characteristic of women who work as full-time journalists which is that they are less likely than male journalists to have children, a disparity which successive surveys have highlighted (Johnston, 2003). And furthermore those female journalists who do have families and reach senior levels very often have what are still considered to be non-standard domestic arrangements.

All the literature demonstrates that there is a steady movement of mothers out of full-time journalism and into part-time or freelance roles. It is particularly those women who have been in full-time *newsroom* roles who tend to move away after they have a family. The interview evidence indicates that, if they are in features roles or magazines, they are more likely to continue in some form once they return from maternity leave. And as discussed in the previous chapters, the clustering of women in these areas of journalism is partly prompted by the choice of lifestyle because they perceive it as more regular, predictable, and therefore family friendly (Williams, 2010).

Jan Howarth referred to wholesale movement of mothers away from full-time journalism as the Sliding Glass Door syndrome rather than the Glass Ceiling (Howarth, 2000). Her study of radio news journalists who followed this path concluded that 'radio news offers good careers opportunities for girls and young women but it is ageist, class conscious and incompatible with motherhood'. So women do fine until they become pregnant, whereupon there is a danger that they will exit the newsroom through the sliding glass door, through which they may not return and, if they do, it is often with reduced prospects. Although Howarth's study focused on radio, where the paucity of women remains a problem (Sound Women, 2013), but sliding glass doors are certainly evident elsewhere in the news.

By Jeremy Gerlis

Hilly Janes had senior staff positions in national newspapers (including the *Guardian, The Times,* and the *Independent*) and then left to go freelance. She is one of many women who have taken this path and who view the high-level media newsroom jobs as 'all consuming'. It is not a matter of prejudice but the nature of running a digital 24/7 operation, which is what these roles now consist of, and which demands a commitment and involvement that excludes most of the rest of life. 'The pressures on journalists to do everything, to update the blogs and twitter feed, to keep the website constantly updated . . . editors on papers and magazines get driven insane, they may have great ideas but it is all squeezed as they have to do so many jobs.'[2] Ann Spackman, a former comment editor at *The Times,* echoes this view. When she did a stint as managing editor she was surprised not by the number of women asking for advice on how to get top jobs – they had the confidence – but on how they could achieve some kind of work–life balance at the same time. She had to point out: 'That it is tough at the top and getting tougher.'

> The Times *first edition used to go off stone at 8.30 and now it is 10.30. The days when you could hop in a cab home at 6pm, put your kids to bed and return later to do the same to the paper are long gone. Digital media stay up all night. And they are greedy . . . Facebook and Twitter need constant feeding. There are blogs to write and iPad editions to create – that happens overnight and 90% of the subs who produce it at* the Times *are men. That is hardly compatible with work/life balance. (Janes, 2011)*

This relentless pressure both as a newsroom reporter or as a senior editorial figure is something that many women struggle with once they have a family. Sue Ellicott, who reluctantly took the decision to go freelance after successful jobs in print and TV, observes that 'all sorts of things trip you up, you are just not aware of them at 21 but they arise at 40'. Bibi van der Zee, a former *Guardian* staffer and now freelancer whose passion remains stories on environmental activism, felt (with three children) constantly hampered in comparison with young single colleagues. 'These kind of stories take hours and involve a huge commitment – running around all over the place, taking risks, whereas it is so easy to be forced into "the homes and garden ghetto"'.[3] Claire McDonald enjoyed working for twelve years in full-time newspaper journalism and she saw plenty of female section editors, but 'they looked stressed and awful. There was no slack in their lives and I thought I don't want to be like you when I have children.' Glenda Cooper as a young enthusiastic reporter on the *Independent* recalls a (rare female) managing editor complaining how 'all the women disappear at a certain level' and resolving to herself that 'I am not going to be like that'. But sure enough she, like many other women, found it preferable to leave her post at a national newspaper and rearrange her career after having children.

One of the most high-profile leavers was the former *Observer* political editor Gaby Hinsliff who had a moment of realisation in 2009 when she resigned and wrote a powerful heartfelt spread, 'I Had it All But I Didn't Have a Life', about how she could no longer manage to juggle. It was a siren call from a woman who grew up long after the early achievements of second-wave feminism – she had had decent maternity leave, an excellent education, and plenty of encouragement, ending in the dream job as a political editor. But in the end the incompatibility of the demands of that, of keeping on top of inconveniently breaking news, drove her to seek a different way of life. Hinsliff announced that she would be starting a blog, www.usedtobesomebody.com.

It is an awkward fact and Hinsliff herself struggled publicly with this feeling of somehow failing to measure up. But many women find the intense demands of news reporting and rising up the editorial greasy pole simply too difficult to combine with family life. This feeds directly into much wider debates about the socialisation of women in contemporary Western society and the extent to which they are expected or want to take on a greater role in caring. Sometimes these concerns erupt into a fierce media battle – for example, when Maeve Haran, a former journalist, left her full-time job and wrote a novel about juggling, *Having It All*, or Nicola Horlick, the city superwoman, wrote *Can You Have It All?* The 2012 version of this was the lively response to Anne-Marie Slaughter's *Atlantic* article 'Why Women Still Can't Have it All'. On each occasion (and on many more) there is a raging debate across the media on the rights and wrongs of mothers with demanding careers. Journalism is not the only career that inspires this kind of frenzy (Horlick was in the City and Slaughter was in politics, working for Hillary Clinton). But the traditional style of how journalism is practised has certain demands that precipitate this extreme tension between workplace and domestic arrangements. In 2013 women still find difficulties in reaching the highest levels in many other areas – politics, the law, business, etc. And there is ongoing evidence that their progress has fallen back in some of these areas (Counting Women In, 2013). Journalism is not an isolated case – but what may make it more inhospitable for mothers is that it is relentless, unpredictable, highly competitive, and dependent upon external agendas. The problem of long hours was confirmed in the most recent survey of the UK journalism workforce which shows that overall journalists work longer hours than the average and over a fifth of journalists work what are considered very long hours (more than 46 hours per week; NCTJ, 2013).

The subject of so-called 'working mothers' has been pored over in the academic literature, in particular the contested work of the sociologist Catherine Hakim, and also frequently raised in the policy area; in recent years by the journalist Cristina Odone's Centre for Policy Studies pamphlet *What Women Want* (Odone, 2009) or the Policy Exchange report *Little Britons* (Mitchell, 2008). Yet there is a special resonance when these debates involve the working lives of journalists because so much of the rhetoric and the debate takes place through the prism of the media, where the topic of working mothers has a continued fascination.

Very often it is the judgemental (verging on unpleasant) tone of the rants on either side between mothers who do and mothers who don't which is particularly noticeable. It is not just that the question barely arises for men, but there is no equivalent judgement of men being viewed as making good and bad or right and wrong choices.

Nevertheless, some mothers do continue in journalism in very demanding full-time roles – but a disproportionate number of those who reach the highest and busiest levels are either childless[4] – like the deputy editor of the *Guardian*, the recent heads of BBC News and of BBC Newsgathering or several leading correspondents across the media. Alternatively they have what are still considered to be unconventional domestic arrangements – such as a non-working partner at home. Michelle Lalor who has edited the *Grimsby Evening Telegraph* for ten years says her life would otherwise have been unthinkable.[5] Similarly in broadcasting there are several women who have adopted this kind of arrangement – for example, Lorraine Heggessey, who held a succession of senior editorial positions culminating in becoming the first woman to run BBC 1, or Alex Crawford, the Sky News foreign correspondent. But this is still viewed as unorthodox, in a society where it remains against social norms for male partners to downshift, for women to 'marry down' and earn more than their non-working partner, and for dads to attend playgroups or wait at the school gate.

The other route is for women to take what is still considered the norm for most men: accept that they are not going to see their children very much – and hand them over to paid childcare. This was the scenario famously fictionalised by the former *Daily Mail* columnist Allison Pearson in *I Don't Know How She Does it.*

These ongoing dilemmas about how to combine a fast-paced life in journalism with nurturing a family, which play out both on an individual as well as a societal level, mean that the dividing line for most women in journalism is that of motherhood. Just as Jana Bennett spoke about a bamboo ceiling, in another sense it has become an elastic ceiling, where those women who, for whatever reason, are not hampered by domestic concerns are able to do well within the traditional media framework. If they can cope with the relentless juggernaut of news, combined with the infinite appetite of digital media plus the standard requirement for work-inspired socialising in their 'spare time', then they might have a reasonable chance of success.

3.3 New ways to work

The most interesting outcome of women's continuing inability to 'choose' is the interaction this has had with some of the possibilities of new media – in relation both to consumption and production. Previously mothers left the full-time workplace and embraced the mummy track, writing articles from home or taking a gentler and usually lower status part-time role, if they could find it. Today's freelancer can do things very differently. She can curate, edit, and crucially reinvent herself as a brand, all from the kitchen table. Gaby Hinsliff has been much admired in this. She has continued to practise journalism, but it is very much on her own terms, using digital and social media to successfully promote her brand. And she has blended a style of political journalism with a wider agenda – very different from the standard Westminster Lobby product. Her book *Half a Wife*, her blog, and crucially her Twitter feed where she calls herself a 'political commentator, downshifter, upshifting if I can just work out which way is up' with over 29,000 followers. That already exceeds the circulation of a political magazine like the *New Statesman*.

Hinsliff is only one example of a whole new evolving genre. Judith O'Reilly was a political producer on *Newsnight* and *Channel 4 News* and later *Sunday Times* education correspondent. She left her job and started a hugely popular blog, www.wifeinthenorth.com, published a book with the same title, and created a brand for herself. Claire McDonald left a successful career at *The Times* after her second child and set up a blog based on children and food, www.crumbsfood.co.uk. Together with her sister (a former broadcast journalist), working from the spare bedroom she has created a popular, growing brand which is beginning to have spin-offs, win awards, and has been featured on Channel 4. Yet it relies on their essential journalism training of reporting, writing, and editing skills to make the subject authentic and interesting. They are cautious about tie-ups with commercial products and careful about picking the right partners. Together with thousands of other so-called 'mummybloggers' they are inventing a new way of finding and communicating with audiences.

Many of the bloggers in turn coalesce around larger networks. The Mumsnet website which has grown into a major media product has a network for bloggers which is in itself a powerful and well-organised product; featuring a sell-out blogfest with multiple sessions on SEO (Search Engine Optimisation), using social media effectively, changing the world, dealing with trolls, and pep talks by a selection of blogging superstars. But Mumsnet are not the only ones. Jen Howze, a former *Times* lifestyle editor has set up www.britmums.com, with 3,000 members and billed as the UK's leading network of parent bloggers, also with its own blogfest for over 500 participants.

The bloggers, brands, and websites based around networks like this are examples of new forms of journalism. The Mumsnet website has a huge range of content for its communities; from Latin lessons to breast-feeding tips. It generates 50 million page views and nearly 7 million visits per month. Some critics argue that they are following a relentlessly lightweight, lifestyle agenda and part of a downward spiral. Yet many of the bloggers and the websites do engage with more serious political topics – discussing benefit changes, campaigning on legal aid cuts, or domestic violence. Leading politicians understand the value of these outlets and are queuing up to participate on their forums.

In various ways this reinvention of journalism, through social networking and new media platforms, has given many women a whole new life outside the more traditional frameworks. But the picture is not entirely rosy. Whilst the social media queen Caitlin Moran might be making a fortune, things are pretty precarious for the freelancer who is dipping her toe in the new media pond. Monetising a blog and creating a brand is not straightforward and many women hoping to find a professional and profitable outlet are reliant, at least in the early stages, upon finding paid work from legacy media. And here the picture is not great. The convulsions of the newspaper industry and the move towards more casualisation have driven far more journalists out of staff jobs (Ornebring, 2009) to fend for themselves, so competition is tough and freelance rates have been in freefall. They are far lower today than they were in the early 1990s. There are recurring problems with freelancers being paid late and treated badly by large media organisations and not everyone can adapt to the insecurity and uncertainty. Many women, who are leaving staff positions at a 'substantially faster pace than men' (Massey & Elmore, 2011), feel that they are entering an electronic cage with increased pressures, rather than enjoying a more congenial life in the freelance electronic cottage.

There is also a darker aspect to the new online world of social media, which many women have been so adept at entering. Female journalists have observed that the problem of (usually anonymous) online abuse or internet trolling is far worse than for their male counterparts. As soon as they veer away from anodyne subjects, women are liable to savage and unpleasant (very often personal) attacks in below the line comments or social media.[6] An article about this tendency in 2013, 'I'm Coming to Rape You Bitch', highlighted some gruesome (almost unprintable) examples (Thompson, 2013).

Helen Lewis, deputy editor of the *New Statesman*, whose job includes moderating online comments, observes that: 'My male colleagues get abuse, and they think that they know what it's like. But it's not the same type of abuse, it's not directed at the same things, and it doesn't tend to be at the same intensity.' One commenter 'called for my fingers to be chopped off', *Evening Standard* columnist Rosamund Urwin has written. 'Another asked if I could go and jump off a cliff because the world would be better for it.' 'Men get told they're stupid, women get told they're ugly', says feminist blogger and columnist Laurie Penny (Thompson, 2013).

According to Lewis and others, some female journalists are so intimidated by this kind of anonymous and unpleasant personal abuse that they are deterred from dealing with more controversial topics (Thompson, 2013). Many female journalists have adapted and benefited greatly in the world of social media – but these torrents of anonymous abuse illustrate that there is a negative side to this. Just as Candy Crowley attracted disproportionate and highly personal attacks after her participation in the presidential debates in 2012, so many less prominent female journalists encounter a version of the same experience. Yet the inventiveness of social media has in turn produced a response to this. A popular Tumblr site 'Said to Lady Journos' has been a way of retaliating and it has gathered a healthy worldwide following by disseminating examples of the kind of offensive online and offline comments which many women receive.[7]

The glass ceiling inhibiting women from the top strata of journalism has not disappeared, but it has changed. Family responsibilities have become a dividing line for those who are not progressing to the senior levels because they are unable or unwilling to commit to long and antisocial hours. But it is not quite so straightforward – after all, nursing means working long hours, on shifts, with stress and emergencies. But no one says women (mothers) cannot cope with the demands of being a nurse. So beyond these obvious constraints there are still areas of residual resistance to women's advancement which perpetuate the sense of a boys' club within traditional media organisations. Yet the encouraging news is that where women are moving into all kinds of new ways of producing and consuming journalism they have been able to flourish. They can introduce a new voice and a new way of interacting with the audience and this is not only good for individuals but it is helping to transform the terms of public discourse.

4

A Feminised News Agenda

Representation of the world, like the world itself, is the work of men: they describe it from their own point of view, which they confuse with the absolute truth. (Simone de Beauvoir, *The Second Sex*, 1949)

4.1 The rise of lifestyle

It was in the 1980s that women first began to make real inroads into journalism. That coincided with deregulation and widening choice for consumers. In the UK this in turn was driven by the Wapping revolution, leading to the expansion of what was available in print, whilst at the same time more TV channels were being launched and they were broadcasting for longer hours. The result was enhanced opportunities within the industry, many of which were taken by women. At the same time there was a huge expansion of 'lifestyle' journalism; more supplements, colour magazines, daytime TV shows, all following this agenda. And correspondingly there has been a lively debate in the literature about whether the postmodern shift to infotainment was the outcome of a 'feminisation' of news (Chambers et al., 2004; Zoonen, 1998). Did the arrival of more women journalists inspire this kind of agenda and lead to a more feminised media? Alternatively, there is considerable evidence that it was the drive by advertisers to attract more female readers and viewers which led to the promotion and expansion of these kinds of journalism (Christmas, 2008).

In 1903 the *Daily Mirror* was established by Harmsworth (later Lord Northcliffe) as 'a newspaper for women run by women . . . a mirror on feminine life' – but that did not last long and after a shaky start all the female journalists were sacked within the year. 'Women can't write and don't want to read' was Northcliffe's sour comment (Holland, 1998).

Yet the idea of appealing to those readers who are the principal family shoppers continued to interest proprietors. When newspapers sought to expand through this lifestyle route, and also when they sought to prop up declining figures by reaching out to a feminine readership, women journalists stood to benefit. Most of the women who went on to become editors of UK national papers in the late 1980s and 1990s were appointed for their experience in this genre – and it is particularly in the Sunday tabloid market that they made their mark. Wendy Henry, Eve Pollard, Patsy Chapman, Tina Weaver, Bridget Rowe, Rebekah Brooks – almost all the women who have edited national papers in the UK – have been employed, at least initially, to run Sunday tabloids and they have arrived there from the lifestyle/magazine areas of journalism, not the news beat.[1] The kind of content they sought brought more opportunities further down the scale – with new innovations such as the ubiquitous 'confessional' columnists, which became such a huge part of journalism at that time and has now evolved on the web, which is so well suited to this kind of outpouring of intimacy. But not all women journalists were pleased at having to pursue this particular agenda. The veteran reporter Auriol Stevens complained in a lecture in 1998 that 'women are relegated to the areas seen as sensational, intrusive, prurient and silly'.

Zoe Heller, the columnist turned novelist, wrote amusingly about the standard types of 'girl writing': the amusing despatches from the home front, the stern comments from a feminist perspective, and the daffy girl confiding on the vagaries of life – most famously epitomised in Bridget Jones. But the more serious point is the extent to which there can be a discernible feminine sensibility within journalism, which might be missing when there are insufficient women participating.

When Jill Abramson became executive editor of the New York Times in 2011 she denied that there was such a thing. But there are plenty of voices who would disagree. For example, a study analysing coverage of the HPV vaccine demonstrated how the priority given to the topic was influenced by the gender make-up of the newsroom (Correa & Harp, 2011). Those publications with a higher proportion of female staff were inclined to give the story more prominence. Even the contemporary focus now on rape as a weapon of war is attributed to the increased number of female conflict reporters. And a number of studies have focused upon the Sarasota Herald in Florida, believed to be the first paper to have an entirely female (five-person) senior management team,[2] under the editorship of Janet Weaver.[3] Building upon the arguments by Zelizer and others that journalists as individuals may influence news content (Zelizer, 2005), what these and other ethnographies and surveys reveal is that when there is a greater preponderance of female editorial figures, it is detectable that there will be a slight shift in news priorities as well as the style of newsgathering and culture in the newsroom (Everbach, 2006; Ricchiardi, 2001). But the extent to which gender differences affect the news agenda is still subject to vigorous and ongoing debate (Liao & Lee, 2013; Reich, 2013).

4.2 Who is making the news?

What is most revealing about the potential difference that women can make is not just in the news agenda but in the increased use of female sources, experts, and voices (Poynter, 2013b). For it is not only by-lines which are male-dominated, but the content of news. The 2012 Women in Journalism Front Page survey, for example, found that, of the 668 people mentioned and quoted, 84% were men. And mostly the women who did feature were either there as victims of crime or because they had married a prince. The front-page quotes were also disaggregated to find out in what capacity subjects were being quoted. Unsurprisingly men were far more likely to be quoted as an expert and women as a victim (WIJ, 2012).

Studies across the world continue to show that the content of news stories is overwhelmingly male. There is a regular five-year study by the Global Media Monitoring Project, 'Who Makes the News?', which started in 1995 and the most recent survey in 2010 reported a gender split of 76/24 across the news stories in 108 countries (GMMP, 2010). Yet in some places things are much worse. In Cambodia women outnumber men in the population and the workforce is 55% female. Yet only 6% of media stories featured women as subjects (Gill, 2007: 115). And even in Scandinavia, where there are plenty of women participating in public life, they were under-represented in the news.

There is a wide literature on the representation of women in the news, a subject which ranges beyond the scope of just the media, as it also questions the values of a wider society where women are not so often doing what are considered to be important or interesting things. However, the question of female experts is very much under the control of those making the programmes or writing the articles. And there is evidence to show from successive reports by the Gender Media Monitoring Project that female journalists are more likely to quote and to rely upon female experts and sources (GMMP, 2010) and thereby to challenge stereotypes in their reporting (Kamerick, 2011). If the media are to achieve a more diverse and inclusive perspective, then this is an obvious starting point (Poynter, 2013b). In the UK several recent campaigns have highlighted the gap and are trying to address it: www.broadcastnow.co.uk/home/expert-women[4] and thewomensroom.org.uk. This issue has become part of a wider national debate in the UK, especially after there was some embarrassment when the BBC's *Today* programme on two consecutive days in October 2012 broadcast a discussion about teenage contraception and then one about breast cancer, neither of which featured any female voice. And the same issue is being highlighted in the US (Women's Media Center, 2012). One survey analysing six months of the 2012 election coverage showed that media discussions of 'women's topics', abortion, birth control, and planned parenthood, were five times as likely to feature male experts (Daily Beast, 2012). If men are being consulted in far greater numbers even on these kinds of topics, then it is hardly surprising if women's voices are not getting much exposure across the media overall.

4.3 Future trends

Unsurprisingly the places where women are doing better in journalism are those with well-regulated workplaces and high levels of encouragement for mothers to work – in particular the Nordic countries – where national policies mean there is a proactive attitude towards equality and gender monitoring. However, even here there is still an imbalance at the higher level favouring men and an ongoing gender pay gap.

It is paradoxical that in parts of Eastern Europe gender proportions in the media are completely different from Western countries. The majority of journalists are female and women predominate in some countries, such as Russia, Latvia, and Bulgaria, even at the highest levels of the media (IWMF, 2011). The head of the Russian organisation of investigative journalists Galina Sidorova[5] points to the distinguished record of female journalists; most famously Anna Politkovskaya – murdered for her reporting on Chechnya. And she attributes the high proportions of women in journalism (80% of Russian journalists are female) to low pay. 'Men prefer to go into big companies or into Public Relations where the pay is better.'[6] And the IFJ report on the gender pay gap in journalism confirmed that Russian journalists are particularly badly paid (Central

European Labour Studies Institute and Wage Indicator Foundation, 2012). This is the classic syndrome where women cluster in the low-paid and therefore low-status areas of the labour market.

In other East European countries the perception is that journalism had a historically low status, as a legacy of Communism (Nastasia, 2013). When journalism, given the constraints of an authoritarian regime, was little more than a state enterprise for rewriting or broadcasting government press releases, it was not accorded the same kind of value or trust as in democratic societies and so became a kind of 'velvet ghetto in Eastern Europe which in turn pulled wages down'.[7] In the former East Germany, after reunification the relative pay and status of the role changed and within a decade the female share of journalism jobs dropped from 60% to 38% (Gallagher, 2008). Yet in other East European countries women have continued to prevail in journalism at all levels – but this is often linked to the enduring low status of the media as an institution in the post-Communist period, combined with relatively low rates of pay.

As journalism has become more insecure and less well remunerated in many Western countries, with the upheaval of digital media, there have been some concerns that this will lead to a wider feminisation along the lines of East European countries. Anecdotally there is evidence of senior male journalists in the UK gravitating towards the highly paid PR sector, as former tabloid editors such as Neil Wallis or David Yellend have done. In that case, just as in Russia, the gender balance may eventually become more female for reasons of pay.

It could also be that the two-tier model which Bob Franklin first identified in *Newszak and News Media* might intersect with the feminisation of the 'lower orders' – the editorial assistants, those doing rewrites of PR material, etc. – which he described as distinct from the top-quality talent (Franklin, 1997). At present this bifurcation does not appear to be happening, beyond the easily identifiable pink ghettoes which have always been women's areas. Given that successive majority cohorts of female journalism students are entering the job market, it would be a useful and illuminating exercise to study more systematically where they find themselves 5, 10, and 20 years later.

The limitations upon women's progress into journalism and as media decision-makers are most apparent in the more traditional spheres. Where the styles of production and the approach to content are least changed then women have in general been less able to make an impact.

51

But when they have carved out new niches, either in the way media are disseminated or in expanding the agenda, then overall they have had the most success. Again it would be useful to pursue research on the way that female entrepreneurs are exploiting the digital revolution, without the constraints of traditional media experience in the newsroom and the wider workplace.

5

Conclusions and Recommendations

The previous chapters have raised a range of issues, begging the obvious question of what needs to be done to make Arnold Bennett's remarks about realising the full potential of women journalists a reality. Tackling some of the disparities faced by women in journalism involves a variety of adjustments: legislative, cultural, highlighting good practice. But, as listed below, in many areas the necessary change involves no more than raising awareness of the problem, often through counting or measuring. And most importantly there needs to be a sustained and conscious effort so that new habits and patterns become embedded, rather than just isolated examples:

- Some of the hurdles faced by women working in journalism are difficult to disentangle from the wider context. In particular those countries and environments where it is difficult for mothers to participate fully in the workplace present a greater challenge for female journalists. The solutions are pretty obvious, they include: a well-regulated workplace, with policies such as non-transferable parental leave; equal pay audits to uncover disparities in remuneration; and fair and transparent recruitment processes. Similar policies already exist in many Nordic countries and elsewhere, especially in the publicly funded media, and the results have started to demonstrate how to achieve a more balanced workforce.
- The latest feminist polemic from Facebook's COO Sheryl Sandberg urges women to 'lean in' and make the most of their opportunities (Sandberg, 2013). But this in turn has provoked reactions about the responsibility of institutions to facilitate life for their female employees. Some organisations have already introduced targets in their recruitment, especially at senior levels, although there is a vigorous debate on whether this is appropriate and if so where the target should be set. At the very least in those areas where women

are almost unrepresented at the higher levels it is worth having the discussion about whether targets might be a solution, albeit just a temporary one.

- Aside from these wider cultural shifts there are identifiable levers which could be used to extend the prospects for female journalists but also to expand horizons for consumers of the media. One way is to increase awareness of the stereotyping and typecasting, so that there is less of a gender divide in types of journalism. Men are unlikely to want to write the make-up tips in *Cosmopolitan* but beyond this there are many areas where it would enhance the product if there was less of a traditional gender divide in the allocation of stories – for example, in the way that women have forged a new style of reporting conflicts. A conscious effort by editors and managers not to succumb to the segregated horizontal workplaces would enhance the prospects for everyone. The recent appointment of Fleet Street's first female sports editor is an encouraging start.

- The age profile in the developed world creeps steadily higher and age discrimination legislation is now accepted in many advanced industrial countries. Against this background a specific campaign to include older women in visible journalistic roles would lead to a more balanced workforce. The representation of both genders should mirror the wider population. There is no reason why on-screen presenters of one gender may carry on until their seventies, whilst the other disappears at 40.

- Online anonymous abuse is an unpleasant side effect of new media, whether manifested in article comments or on Twitter, and female journalists are disproportionately targeted. Current efforts to use technology and thereby prevent anonymity or regulatory and legal means to highlight and stamp on such practice would be welcomed by those who are on the receiving end of this behaviour and create a pleasanter public space for everyone.

- The drift from staff to freelance positions by many women in journalism, especially after they have become mothers, is a well-travelled path. But freelance rates have collapsed over the past two decades due to other pressures in journalism and there is a continual problem in the way that freelancers across the media are treated by large organisations. Any measures to introduce better practice here, in particular to ensure that freelancers are given due recognition and do not have to wait months for payment, would directly improve the position of the large number of women freelance journalists.

• Enhancing the prospects of women in journalism is part of a better gender balance right across public life. And one way in which the media can reinforce this overall pattern is to work harder to portray women as experts and contributors. There has been plenty of work done to highlight the imbalances here and there are very straightforward ways in which it is possible to change the status quo. Ultimately the news agenda can be diversified and made more appealing to audiences by widening the range of voices – not always going to the same traditional opinions, both as contributors and producers. And that in turn depends upon a more diverse workforce.

All those familiar prescriptions for achieving greater gender equality, in particular the requirement for more transparency, are as relevant to journalism as to other workplaces. Yet beyond this, newsgathering and production, as they are currently constituted, are bound to be intensive and all-absorbing enterprises. In which case, if women are to be fully involved, this depends upon wider social adjustment about how working and caring are incorporated in twenty-first-century lives. And here the media as a whole can certainly be a catalyst in provoking and enhancing the debate.

Appendices

Appendix 1

By-line research week beginning 1 October 2012

Daily Mail	Mon 1-10		Tue 2-10		Wed 3-10		Thu 4-10		Fri 5-10		Sat 6-10		Sun 7-10	
	M	F	M	F	M	F	M	F	M	F	M	F	M	F
UK	14	1	16	4	11	5	9	4	13	2	21	4	15	5
Politics	6	–	7	3	8	–	8	1	10	1	8	–	12	2
World	2	2	1	–	1	–	1	1	2	–	6	–	3	1
Business/finance	2	–	8	4	15	7	15	–	8	1	7	2	33	14
Sports	27	1	16	1	20	2	22	1	22	–	22	–	29	2
Health/social	–	3	1	11	1	2	2	4	–	2	–	–	1	8
Entertainment/celebs	3	–	2	4	4	–	6	2	6	4	9	9	14	3
Culture/arts	–	–	–	–	–	–	–	–	–	–	–	–	1	–
Environment/science	2	–	1	–	–	–	1	1	1	1	1	1	4	–
Life & style	3	8	2	3	2	4	4	12	1	1	2	2	7	17 Prop†1
Total	59	15	54	30	62	20	68	26	63	24	76	18	119	53

† Property, interior design

59

By-line research week beginning 1 October 2012

Telegraph	Mon 1-10		Tue 2-10		Wed 3-10		Thu 4-10		Fri 5-10		Sat 6-10		Sun 7-10	
	M	F	M	F	M	F	M	F	M	F	M	F	M	F
UK	7	6	11	5	12	6	12	4	12	5	12	3	9	2
Politics	12	2	9	–	7	2	8	3	12	2	5	1	17	–
World	8	3	10	3	14	–	8	1	21	2	17	–	9	1
Business/finance	15	13	14	12	14	13	16	10	13	11	13	9	18	6
Sports	30	–	29	–	31	1	27	–	24	–	21	–	30	1
Health/social	1	3	6	2	5	1	5	–	1	1	4	3	1	1
Entertainment/celebs	5	1	2	2	1	2	1	1	8	2	11	3	5	1
Culture/arts	4	1	3	2	–	1	3	–	2	2	3	2	5	4
Environment/science	1	1	2	1	–	2	2	2	–	3	5	2	2	2
Life & style	1	1	–	1	TFD* –	1	TFD 1	–	1	–	3	8	2	2
													TFD 3	7
													Prop† 1	2
Total	84	31	86	28	79	30	83	23	94	28	94	31	92	29

* Travel, food, drink
† Property, interior design

By-line research week beginning 1 October 2012

Sun	Mon 1-10		Tue 2-10		Wed 3-10		Thu 4-10		Fri 5-10		Sat 6-10		Sun 7-10	
	M	F	M	F	M	F	M	F	M	F	M	F	M	F
UK	11	3	13	3	15	3	15	6	17	4	12	3	14	4
Politics	–	–	2	–	1	1	6	1	5	2	2	2	5	–
World	6	3	–	–	1	–	1	–	–	–	2	1	5	–
Business/finance	–	–	2	1	1	1	–	–	2	–	1	–	1	1
Sports	39	1	16	–	28	–	19	–	16	–	44	2	46	1
Health/social	–	–	–	1	1	–	–	1	–	–	–	1	2	–
Entertainment/celebs	5	1	9	3	9	–	7	5	9	3	14	1	8	2
Culture/arts	1	–	1	–	–	1	–	–	1	–	–	–	–	–
Environment/science	–	–	–	–	–	2	–	–	3	–	2	–	1	–
Life & style	1	3	–	2	–	–	–	3	1	–	1	3	2	8
Total	63	11	43	10	56	8	48	16	54	9	78	13	84	16

By-line research week beginning 1 October 2012

Independent	Mon 1-10		Tue 2-10		Wed 3-10		Thu 4-10		Fri 5-10		Sat 6-10		Sun 7-10	
	M	F	M	F	M	F	M	F	M	F	M	F	M	F
UK	8	3	5	6	13	2	15	2	15	2	11	–	5	5
Politics	8	–	10	–	8	–	8	1	6	–	7	–	6	6
World	9	1	6	2	8	–	9	2	11	–	10	3	2	3
Business/finance	8	2	10	2	11	6	15	2	12	5	21	3	9	6
Sports	20	1	18	–	21	–	21	–	20	–	26	1	36	2
Health/social	–	2	1	1	–	–	–	1	1	2	1	–	–	2
Entertainment/celebs	1	–	3	1	3	1	1	1	2	1	2	3	2	4
Culture/arts	1	4	1	2	4	2	4	1	3	–	13	6	4	1
Environment/science	2	–	2	–	2	–	4	1	3	–	2	–	2	–
Life & style	1	3	3	4	–	5	–	3	–	–	3	3	2	1
TFD*	1	1	–	2					2	2	5	3	4	3
Prop†											–	2	–	3
Total	59	17	59	20	70	16	77	14	75	12	101	23	72	36

* Travel, food, drink
† Property, interior design

By-line research week beginning 1 October 2012

The Times	Mon 1-10		Tue 2-10		Wed 3-10		Thu 4-10		Fri 5-10		Sat 6-10		Sun 7-10	
	M	F	M	F	M	F	M	F	M	F	M	F	M	F
UK	7	4	8	5	12	6	14	5	19	6	8	4	14	3
Politics	4	2	2	3	5	2	3	2	5	3	5	2	15	4
World	10	4	10	1	12	3	9	2	9	4	13	4	10	5
Business/finance	13	4	17	1	22	3	17	3	25	4	19	7	32	12
Sports	49	–	25	–	30	–	25	1	29	2	31	3	43	–
Health/social	2	–	2	2	1	–	1	–	–	–	3	4	4	4
Entertainment/celebs	2	–	1	–	3	–	1	1	2	–	3	4	4	4
Culture/arts	2	–	1	1	4	–	3	1	4	–	6	2	21	4
Environment/science	–	–	1	–	–	–	1	–	1	–	7	1	8	4
Life & style	2	3	–	2	–	6	Law 3	2	Prop† 1	9	TFD* 4	1	5	15
													Motor 4	–
													Prop 3	7
													TFD 12	4
Total	91	17	67	15	89	18	78	18	95	28	101	41	175	66

* Travel, food, drink
† Property, interior design

By-line research week beginning 26 November 2012

Telegraph	Mon 26-11		Tue 27-11		Wed 28-11		Thu 29-11		Fri 30-11		Sat 1-12		Sun 2-12	
	M	F	M	F	M	F	M	F	M	F	M	F	M	F
UK	8	6	10	2	12	2	11	1	14	2	17	–	16	4
Politics	7	3	10	2	8	3	11	3	14	2	9	1	5	1
World	7	1	14	2	7	2	16	1	18	1	14	1	5	2
Business/finance	10	13	9	7	16	9	16	10	17	9	19	11	16	16
Sports	38	–	28	–	24	2	27	–	25	–	33	1	35	–
Health/social	2	4	3	–	2	–	5	–	1	–	3	–	–	3
Entertainment/celebs	5	3	3	4	1	2	6	3	4	2	2	3	4	2
Culture/arts	2	1	3	2	3	2	3	1	2	1	1	1	4	3
Environment/science	2	1	3	3	–	1	2	–	1	1	4	1	8	3
Life & style	–	–	TFD* –	1	2	2	2	2	1	1	2	2	3	9
					TFD 1	–	TFD 1	–	TFD 1	–	TFD 1	–	TFD 3	–
													Prop† –	1
Total	81	32	83	25	76	25	100	21	98	19	105	21	99	44

* Travel, food, drink
† Property, interior design

By-line research week beginning 26 November 2012

Independent	Mon 26-11		Tue 27-11		Wed 28-11		Thu 29-11		Fri 30-11		Sat 1-12		Sun 2-12	
	M	F	M	F	M	F	M	F	M	F	M	F	M	F
UK	5	1	16	3	9	3	13	3	27	3	11	2	4	3
Politics	9	1	5	–	4	–	6	–	5	1	10	2	5	3
World	10	1	15	7	13	1	12	1	13	–	14	2	9	1
Business/finance	9	1	10	2	16	2	14	3	15	4	20	4	10	4
Sports	30	1	23	–	17	–	22	–	15	–	24	–	26	1
Health/social	2	–	5	–	4	–	1	2	1	–	4	1	1	2
Entertainment/celebs	2	–	6	6	2	1	2	1	2	–	5	5	3	–
Culture/arts	3	1	2	3	–	3	–	3	–	–	11	7	5	2
Environment/science	3	–	13	3	–	–	2	–	3	–	–	–	4	–
Life & style	1	5	TFD* 7	–	TFD 1	–	1	1	Prop† 1 TFD 1	–	Prop 2 TFD 14	1	TFD 3	3
Total	74	11	103	30	66	11	73	14	83	9	117	32	74	21

* Travel, food, drink
† Property, interior design

65

By-line research week beginning 26 November 2012

The Times	Mon 26-11		Tue 27-11		Wed 28-11		Thu 29-11		Fri 30-11		Sat 1-12		Sun 2-12	
	M	F	M	F	M	F	M	F	M	F	M	F	M	F
UK	7	8	5	2	8	3	14	5	12	5	14	10	15	2
Politics	2	3	6	2	14	2	3	3	6	1	5	2	7	4
World	11	3	9	1	12	2	13	4	15	2	15	5	13	3
Business/finance	14	3	23	7	15	6	23	6	22	7	28	14	36	14
Sports	41	1	25	2	41	–	34	–	39	1	27	2	38	1
Health/social	2	3	7	2	3	1	3	3	4	1	1	2	2	1
Entertainment/celebs	1	–	1	–	–	–	1	–	–	1	4	3	8	2
Culture/arts	2	1	3	1	3	–	1	2	5	1	9	6	17	6
Environment/science	3	1	3	–	1	–	1	–	3	2	4	1	9	2
Life & style	–	2	–	1	1	6	–	4	–	–	1	14	7	11
							Prop†1	–	Prop1	4	Prop 3	–	Prop1	7
							TFD*1	1	TFD –	1	TFD 2	5	TFD 10	4
							Law 3	1						
Total	83	25	82	18	98	20	98	29	107	26	113	64	163	57

* Travel, food, drink
† Property, interior design

By-line research week beginning 26 November 2012

Sun	Mon 26-11		Tue 27-11		Wed 28-11		Thu 29-11		Fri 30-11		Sat 1-12		Sun 2-12	
	M	F	M	F	M	F	M	F	M	F	M	F	M	F
UK	10	1	11	1	13	1	13	2	13	5	15	2	13	2
Politics	1	4	4	–	4	–	18	5	12	3	4	–	5	–
World	–	–	2	–	4	–	–	1	–	–	1	–	5	–
Business/finance	–	–	2	–	1	2	2	2	5	–	1	–	4	–
Sports	43	1	23	–	38	1	22	1	25	2	52	2	51	2
Health/social	–	2	1	2	–	3	1	4	2	1	–	1	3	1
Entertainment/celebs	7	3	7	4	8	4	5	3	9	6	16	8	7	3
Culture/arts	–	–	–	–	–	–	2	–	2	2	–	–	–	–
Environment/science	1	–	1	–	–	1	3	–	7	–	2	1	2	1
Life & style	2	–	1	2	–	2	2	5	1	1	TFD* 1	1	1	6
													TFD –	
													Prop† –	
Total	64	11	52	9	68	14	68	23	76	20	93	18	91	17

* Travel, food, drink
† Property, interior design

By-line research week beginning 26 November 2012

Daily Mail	Mon 26-11		Tue 27-11		Wed 28-11		Thu 29-11		Fri 30-11		Sat 1-12		Sun 2-12	
	M	F	M	F	M	F	M	F	M	F	M	F	M	F
UK	10	3	13	4	10	4	14	4	19	3	6	4	14	2
Politics	4	–	4	–	7	–	9	–	4	–	7	1	9	1
World	1	–	1	–	1	–	2	–	1	–	2	1	2	1
Business/finance	2	2	10	3	15	8	9	1	9	2	7	1	22	10
Sports	24	–	17	2	19	–	22	–	21	–	22	–	32	1
Health/social	2	2	4	5	2	3	5	2	–	1	2	2	5	8
Entertainment/celebs	5	3	3	3	1	2	2	1	9	2	6	4	5	4
Culture/arts	–	–	–	–	–	2	–	–	–	–	–	–	4	–
Environment/science	1	2	–	2	1	1	3	–	5	2	3	1	2	2
Life & style	2	4	2	2	–	3	4	9	2	2	2	4	2	8
	Prop† 1	–			TFD* 1	–			TFD –	1	TFD 1	–	TFD 7	5
									Prop 1	2			Prop 2	1
Total	52	16	54	21	57	23	70	17	71	15	58	18	106	41

* Travel, food, drink
† Property, interior design

Appendix 2

MHMK Macromedia Hochschule für Medien und Kommunikation

Deutsche Sporthochschule Köln
German Sport University Cologne

Results of ISPS 2011

- sport journalism in international print media is a man's world: more than 90% of the writers are male

- only 8% of the articles by named journalists are written by women

- n=11.123

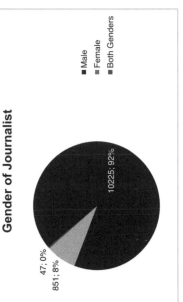

Gender of Journalist

47; 0%

851; 8%

10225; 92%

■ Male
■ Female
■ Both Genders

ISPS 2011 - Prof. Dr. Thomas Horky/Dr. Jörg-Uwe Nieland

Appendix 3

Opinion and comment pieces week beginning 1 October 2012

Daily Mail	Mon 1-10 M	F	Tue 2-10 M	F	Wed 3-10 M	F	Thu 4-10 M	F	Fri 5-10 M	F	Sat 6-10 M	F	Sun 7-10 M	F
Comment and opinion	5	1	3	2	2	1	5	–	5	1	3	2	4	2

Telegraph	Mon 1-10 M	F	Tue 2-10 M	F	Wed 3-10 M	F	Thu 4-10 M	F	Fri 5-10 M	F	Sat 6-10 M	F	Sun 7-10 M	F
Comment and opinion	4	3	7	1	7	1	5	1	6	1	5	2	7	2

The Times	Mon 1-10 M	F	Tue 2-10 M	F	Wed 3-10 M	F	Thu 4-10 M	F	Fri 5-10 M	F	Sat 6-10 M	F	Sun 7-10 M	F
Comment and opinion	6	1	6	3	8	2	6	2	9	3	7	3	16	6

Independent	Mon 1-10 M	F	Tue 2-10 M	F	Wed 3-10 M	F	Thu 4-10 M	F	Fri 5-10 M	F	Sat 6-10 M	F	Sun 7-10 M	F
Comment and opinion	6	3	5	3	5	3	6	2	7	2	8	2	7	4

Sun	Mon 1-10 M	F	Tue 2-10 M	F	Wed 3-10 M	F	Thu 4-10 M	F	Fri 5-10 M	F	Sat 6-10 M	F	Sun 7-10 M	F
Comment and opinion	–	–	1	–	–	1	2	–	1	1	1	1	1	1

Opinion and comment pieces week beginning 26 November 2012

	Mon 26-11		Tue 27-11		Wed 28-11		Thu 29-11		Fri 30-11		Sat 1-12		Sun 2-12	
	M	F	M	F	M	F	M	F	M	F	M	F	M	F
Daily Mail														
Comment and opinion	1	2	4	–	4	1	6	–	5	–	2	2	3	2
Telegraph														
Comment and opinion	5	1	13	1	4	2	8	2	9	1	6	1	11	2
The Times														
Comment and opinion	9	2	7	3	7	2	6	2	11	3	9	2	7	2
Independent														
Comment and opinion	6	2	4	3	8	3	4	2	10	1	11	1	9	3
Sun							Thu 29-11*							
Comment and opinion	1	–	1	–	–	1	15	7	8	3	3	–	2	–

* This was the day that the Leveson report was released, and the *Sun* asked for comments from a wide selection of writers, hence the disproportionate number of contributors.

Notes

Chapter 1   Introduction

1   BBC Written Archive Centre, 'Limitations to the Recruitment and Advancement of Women in the BBC', report presented to BBC Board of Management, BM(73) 31.

2   Interview with the author in 2008 for Jean Seaton's *BBC Official History*, vol. 6 (Profile Books, forthcoming).

3   Interview with the author in 2006 for *BBC Official History*, vol. 6.

4   BBC Written Archive Centre, R 78/2 257/1.

5   The total included written and oral evidence from journalists, editors, proprietors, regulators, academics, and former journalists.

6   The 2012 version of this was sparked off by the Princeton Professor Anne-Marie Slaughter's cover story 'Why Women Still Can't Have it All', in *The Atlantic,* July 2012 (and broke readership records for the magazine's website), explaining why she left her job at the State Department. A furious public row ensued, which included a high-profile response from the Facebook COO Sheryl Sandberg (NY Times/Elite Women): www.nytimes.com/2012/06/22/us/elite-women-put-a-new-spin-on-work-life-debate.html?_r=0.

7   This study in 2012 identified the 17 papers shortlisted in the category 'publication of the year' of the Guardian Student Media Awards. There were 11 women and 9 men (some of the papers had joint editors).

Chapter 2   Where Are the Women?

1   Interview with Professor Karen Ross, Oct. 2012, discussing the project on Women Decision Makers in the Media, a survey of 99 large media organisations across the EU, under the aegis of the European Institute for Gender Equality.

2   See Chapter 4 for more discussion on this.

3　http://politics.co.uk/news/2013/05/16/harman-investigates-mystery-of-missing-older-women-tv-presenters.

4　Margarey Kirk Gatey edited a Northcliffe paper, 1939–43, taking over as proprietor and editor of the *Exeter Express and Echo* upon the death of her father.

5　Northcliffe Group was the largest regional group – but the titles were sold on at the end of 2012.

6　Interview with the author in 2006 for *BBC Official History*, vol. 6.

7　Lynn Barber, whose career included *Penthouse* and the *Sunday Express*, revealed in an interview that the *Independent* was the most sexist place she had ever worked (Dougary, 1994: 100).

8　Interview with the author, Nov. 2012.

9　Interviewed by *Cosmopolitan* in 1990.

10　See *Guardian* (2013), covering reviews published in March 2013, in the UK weekly and daily national press.

11　Interview with the author, Nov. 2012.

Chapter 3　Beyond the Glass Ceiling

1　Interview with the author, Nov. 2012.

2　Interview, Oct. 2012.

3　Interview, Sept. 2012.

4　There has been a steady rise in the proportion of women who remain childless. One in five women in the UK born in 1965, whose childbearing years are probably over, have no children. This proportion has almost doubled from one in nine of women born in 1938: www.ons.gov.uk/ons/dcp171778_247008.pdf.

5　Interview with the author, Dec. 2012.

6　Interview with Elizabeth Day, *Observer* features journalist, Nov. 2012.

7　http://saidtoladyjournos.tumblr.com.

Chapter 4　A Feminised News Agenda

1　This also applies to Lisa Markwell, appointed to edit the *Independent on Sunday* in April 2013.

2　The Legend of Amazonia – as it is referred to – began in 1999.

3   Janet Weaver – like a number of other senior figures in journalism – had a 'stay-at-home' husband; see Chapter 3.

4   The Expert Women campaign is based upon an ongoing research project at City University London which regularly monitors the use of female experts and sources in a range of broadcast news programmes.

5   Galina Sidorova is also the current chair of the International Press Institute.

6   Interview with the author, Nov. 2012.

7   Interview with Professor Karen Ross, Oct. 2012.

References

4th Estate (2012) *Men are Telling the Stories of Election 2012*, 28 Aug., retrieved Dec. 2012, from www.4thestate.net/men-are-telling-the-stories-of-election-2012.

Aldridge, M., and Evetts, J. (2003) 'Rethinking the Concept of Professionalism: The Case of Journalism', *British Journal of Sociology*, 54/4: 547–64.

Avadani, I. (2002) 'From Fashion to Profession: Education of Journalists in Romania', in T. Jusic and M. Dedovic (eds), *Education of Journalists in Southeast Europe: A Step Closer to Professionalism* (Sarajevo: Media Online), 120–35.

Barnett, E. (2012) 'The Unique Advantage of Female War Reporters in Muslim Countries', *www.telegraph.co.uk*, 21 Nov., retrieved Apr. 2013, from www. telegraph.co.uk/women/womens-life/9692810/The-unique-advantage-of-female-war-reporters-in-Muslim-countries.html.

Beasley, M., and Gibbons, S. (2003) *Taking their Place: A Documentary History of Women in Journalism* (Pennsylvania: Strata Publishing).

Beasley, M., and Theus, K. (1988) *The New Majority: A Look at What the Preponderance of Women in Journalism Education Means to the Schools and to the Professions* (New York: University Press of America).

Bennett, A. (1898) *Journalism for Women: A Practical Guide* (London: Bodley Head; available on Kindle).

Broadcast (2012) 'Woman of Achievement', 6 Dec., retrieved Dec. 2012, from www.broadcastnow.co.uk/in-depth/the-broadcast-interview/woman-of-achievement/5049687.article.

Bromley, M. (2009) 'The United Kingdom Journalism Education Landscape', in G. Terzis (ed.), *European Journalism Education* (Bristol: Intellect), 47–66.

Bromley, M. (2013) 'The "New Majority" and the Academization of Journalism', *Journalism: Theory, Practice and Criticism*, forthcoming.

Central European Labour Studies Institute and Wage Indicator Foundation with the support of the International Federation of Journalists (2012) *Gender Pay Gap in Journalism*, retrieved July 2013, from www.ifj.org/assets/docs/196/008/728fdc4-99dbd08.pdf.

Chambers, D., Steiner, L., and Flemming, C. (2004) *Women and Journalism* (London: Routledge).

Christmas, L. (2008) 'Women in Media in the UK', in R. Frohlich and S. Lafky (eds), *Women Journalists in the Western World: What Surveys Tell Us* (Ann Arbor, Mich.: Hampton Press), 123–38.

CJR (2012) 'It's 2012 Already: Why is Opinion Writing Still Mostly Male?', 29 May, retrieved Jan. 2013, from www.cjr.org/behind_the_news/its_2012_already_why_is_opinio.php?page=all.

Cochrane, K. (2011) 'Why is British Public Life Dominated by Men?', 4 Dec., retrieved Dec. 2012, from www.guardian.co.uk/lifeandstyle/2011/dec/04/why-british-public-life-dominated-men.

Collins, G. (2012) 'The Best Mailgirl Ever', *International Herald Tribune*, 29 June.

Colvin, M. (2012) *On the Frontline: The Collected Journalism of Marie Colvin* (London: HarperPress).

Coren, Y., and Negev, E. (2011) *First Lady of Fleet Street: A Biography of Rachel Beer* (London: JR Books).

Correa, T., and Harp, D. (2011) 'Women Matter in Newsrooms: How Power and Critical Mass Relate to the Coverage of the HPV Vaccine', *Journalism and Mass Communication Quarterly*, 88/2: 301–19.

Counting Women In (2013) *Sex and Power: Who Runs Britain?* London: Counting Women In coalition: Centre for Women and Democracy, the Electoral Reform Society, the Fawcett Society, the Hansard Society, and Unlock Democracy.

Cox, G. (2012) 'Where do All the Female Journalists Go?', retrieved Dec. 2012, from http://thatgracecox.tumblr.com/post/34109797037/where-do-all-the-female-journalists-go.

Craft, C. (1991) *Too Old, Too Ugly and Not Deferential to Men: An Anchorwoman's Courageous Battle Against Sex Discrimination* (Roseville, CA: Prima Lifestyle Publishing).

Crouse, T. (1973) *The Boys on the Bus* (New York: Random House).

Daily Beast (2012) 'Men Rule Media Coverage of Women's News', 31 May, retrieved Jan. 2013, from www.thedailybeast.com/articles/2012/05/31/men-rule-media-coverage-of-women-s-news.html.

Daily Mail (2012) 'I got it Wrong on Older Women', 9 Feb., retrieved Dec. 2012, from www.dailymail.co.uk/news/article-2098498/I-got-wrong-older-women-BBC-boss-admits-ARE-TV.html.

Delano, A. (2003) 'Women Journalists: What's the Difference?', *Journalism Studies*, 4/2: 273–86.

Delius, M. (2012) 'European Eye', *Standpoint* (July/Aug.), 25.

Democratic Audit (2012) 'Women in Political Life. How far do Women Participate in Political Life and Public Office at All Levels?', retrieved Dec. 2012, from http://democracy-uk-2012.democraticaudit.com/women-in-political-life.

Dixon, R. (2012) 'Poetry Killed the Radio Star', 21 Sept., retrieved Dec. 2012, from http://ruthedixon.blogspot.com/2012/09/dear-george-i-am-broadcast-journalist.htm.

Dougary, G. (1994) *The Executive Tart and Other Myths: Media Women Talk Back* (London: Virago).

Engstrom, E., and Ferri, A. (1998) 'From Barriers to Challenges: Career Perceptions of Women TV News Anchors', *Journalism and Mass Communication Quarterly*, 75/4: 789–802.

Evening Standard (2012) Interview with Stella Creasy MP, 7 Sept.

Everbach, T. (2006) 'The Culture of a Woman-Led Newspaper', *Journalism and Mass Communication Quarterly*, 83/3: 477–93.

Everbach, T., and Flournoy, C. (2007) 'Women Leave Journalism for Better Pay, Work Conditions', *Newspaper Research Journal*, 28/3: 52–64.

Fahs, A. (2011) *Out on Assignment. Newspaper Women and the Making of the Modern Public Space* (Chapel Hill, NC: University of North Carolina Press).

Franklin, B. (1997) *Newszak and News Media* (London: Hodder Education).

Franks, S. (1999) *Having None of It: Women, Men and the Future of Work* (London: Granta).

Franks, S. (2011) 'Attitudes to Women in the BBC in the 1970s: Not So Much a Glass Ceiling as one of Reinforced Concrete', *Westminster Papers in Culture and Communication*, 8/3: 123–42.

Frohlich, R., and Holtz-Bacha, C. (2008) 'Women in German Journalism: Where do All the Women Go?', in R. Frohlich and S. Lafky (eds), *Women Journalists in the Western World: What Surveys Tell Us* (Ann Arbor, Mich.: Hampton Press).

Gallagher, M. (2008) 'At the Millennium: Shifting Patterns in Gender and Culture', in R. Frolich and S. Lafky (eds), *Women Journalists in the Western World: What Surveys Tell Us* (Ann Arbor, Mich.: Hampton Press).

Gallagher, M. (2001) 'Reporting on Gender in Journalism' (winter), retrieved Dec. 2012, from www.nieman.harvard.edu/reportsitem.aspx?id=101542.

Gill, R. (2007) *Gender and the Media* (Cambridge: Polity).

GMMP (2010) *Who Makes the News?* Global Media Monitoring Project, retrieved Jan. 2013, from http://whomakesthenews.org.

Greenslade, R. (2011) 'Men Still Dominate National Newspaper Journalism', 4 Mar., retrieved Dec. 2012, from www.guardian.co.uk/media/greenslade/2011/mar/04/women-national-newspapers.

Grenby, M. K. (2009) 'Girls, Girls, Girls: A Study of the Popularity of Journalism as a Career among Female Teenagers and its Corresponding Lack of Appeal to Young Males', *Australian Journalism Monographs*, 11/1: 1–44.

Grey, E. (2012) *Women in Journalism at the Fin de Siècle: Making a Name for Herself* (Basingstoke: Palgrave).

Guardian (2011) 'Miriam O'Reilly Celebrates Ageism Victory Against BBC', 11 Jan., retrieved Jan. 2012, from www.guardian.co.uk/media/2011/jan/11/miriam-oreilly-bbc-ageism-victory?intcmp=239.

Guardian (2012a) 'George Entwistle Pledges More Chances for Female Presenters at BBC', 19 Sept., retrieved Dec. 2012, from www.guardian.co.uk/media/2012/sep/19/george-entwistle-bbc-women-presenters?INTCMP=SRCH.

Guardian (2012b) 'Womens Sport is Underfunded and Ignored', 24 Oct., retrieved Dec. 2012, from www.guardian.co.uk/lifeandstyle/2012/oct/24/womens-sport-underfunded-ignored-charity-claims.

Guardian (2013) 'Gender Balancing the Books', 8 June, retrieved July 2013, from www.guardian.co.uk/books/2013/jun/08/gender-balancing-books.

Guardian datablog (2012) 'Women's Representation in Media: The Best Data on the Subject to Date', retrieved July 2013, from www.guardian.co.uk/news/datablog/2012/sep/07/gender-media-best-data-available#data.

Holland, P. (1998) 'The Politics of the Smile: "Soft News" and the Sexualisation of the Popular Press', in C. Carter, G. Branston and S. Allan (eds), *News, Gender and Power* (London: Routledge).

Howarth, J. (2000) 'Women in Radio News: Making a Difference', in C. Mitchell (ed.), *Women and Radio: Airing Differences* (London: Routledge), 250–62.

Huffington Post (2012) 'Hey Internet, Stop Attacking Candy Crowley's Weight', 17 Oct., retrieved Dec. 2012, from www.huffingtonpost.com/emma-gray/candy-crowley-weight-attacks-presidential-debate-moderator_b_1971955.html.

Hunter, F. (1996) 'Teenage Girls as Journalism Students at London University 1919–39', Institute of Contemporary British History conference, London.

Independent (2013) 'Incoming BBC News Director Promises Action for More On-air Female Journalists', 23 May, retrieved June 2013, from www.independent.co.uk/news/media/tv-radio.

INSI (2012) *No Woman's Land: On the Frontlines with Female Reporters* (London: International News Safety Institute).

ISPS (2011) *International Sports Press Survey: Play the Game* (Cologne: Deutsche Sport Hochschule).

IWMF (2011) *Global Report on the Status of Women in the News Media* (Washington, DC: IWMF).

Janes, H. (2011) 'I've Seen the Future and it's Female', *British Journalism Review*, 22/2: 39–44.

Johnston, L. (2003) 'Are there Opportunities for Women to Transcend Gender Organisation in Print Journalism and Do Workplace Policies Allow These Women to Obtain a Work–Life Balance?', University of Strathclyde, M.Litt. thesis.

Journalism Training Forum (2002) *Journalists at Work* (London: Journalism Training Forum).

Kamerick, M. (2011) 'Women Should Represent Women', Sept., retrieved Jan. 2013, from www.ted.com/talks/megan_kamerick_women_should_represent_women_in_media.html.

Lee, F., and Liao, S. (2013) 'Do Journalists Believe in Gender Specificities in News Work? The Impact of Professionalism and Family Life', paper delivered at ICA 2013 Conference, London.

Lonsdale, S. (2013) 'We Agreed that Women were a Nuisance in the Office Anyway', *Journalism Studies*, forthcoming August.

Massey, B., and Elmore, C. (2011) 'Happier Working for Themselves: Job Satisfaction and Women Freelance Journalists', *Journalism Practice*, 5/6: 672–86.

Media Guido (2013) 'Where have All the Women Gone?', 7 Jan., retrieved Jan. 2013, from http://order-order.com/2013/01/07/where-have-all-the-women-gone.

Melki, J. (2009) 'Journalism and Media Studies in Lebanon', *Journalism Studies*, 10/5: 672–90.

Milburn, A. (2012) *Fair Access to Professional Careers* (London: Cabinet Office), ch. 5.

Mitchell, L. (2008) *Little Britons: Financing Childcare Choice* (London: Policy Exchange), retrieved July 2013, from www.policyexchange.org.uk/publications/category/item/little-britons-financing-childcare-choice.

Moran, C. (2011) *How to Be a Woman* (London: Ebury Press).

Murphy, K. (2011) 'On an Equal Footing with Men? Women in the BBC 1922–1939', London, Goldsmiths College, PhD thesis.

Nastasia, D. (2013) 'Bulgaria: Cinderella Went to Market, with Consequences for Women Journalists', in C. M. Byerly (ed.), *Palgrave Handbook of Women and Journalism* (London: Palgrave).

National Council for the Training of Journalists (2013) *Journalists at Work: Their Views on Training, Recruitment and Conditions* (Saffron Walden: NCTJ).

New Matilda (2013) 'Where are the Women in the Media?', http://newmatilda.com/2013/03/08/where-are-women-media.

Newman, C. (2013) 'Where have All the Women Political Journalists Gone?', *Daily Telegraph*, 8 Jan., retrieved Jan. 2013, from www.telegraph.co.uk/women/womens-politics/9787362/Where-have-all-the-women-political-journalists-gone.html.

NUJ (2012) http://union-news.co.uk/2012/10/nuj-condemns-sexism-and-harassment-in-the-media.

Nyondo, R. (2011) *Audit of Gender in Media Education and Training in Southern Africa* (Johannesburg: Gender Links).

O'Reilly, M. (2012) Speech made at Ageism and Sexism in the Media conference.

Odone, C. (2009) *What Women Want: And How They Can Get It* (London: Centre for Policy Studies), retrieved July 2013, from www.cps.org.uk/publications/reports/what-women-want-and-how-they-can-get-it.

Ornebring, H. (2009) *The Two Professionalisms of Journalism* (Oxford: RISJ).

Poindexter, P. (2008) 'Finding Women in the Newsroom and in the News', in P. Poindexter, S. Meraz, and A. Weiss, *Divided and Disconected in the News Media Landscape* (New York: Routledge), 65–85.

Povich, L. (2012) *The Good Girls Revolt: How the Women of Newsweek Sued their Bosses and Changed the Workplace* (New York: Public Affairs).

Poynter (2013a) 'New Media No Better than Old Media When it Comes to Women's Bylines', 22 Feb., retrieved July 2013, from www.poynter.org/latest-news/mediawire/205123/report-new-media-no-better-than-old-media-when-it-comes-to-womens-bylines.

Poynter (2013b) 'Lack of Female Sources in NY Times Front-page Stories Highlights Need for Change', 16 July, retrieved July 2012 from www.poynter.org/latest-news/top-stories/217828/lack-of-female-sources-in-new-york-times-stories-spotlights-need-for-change.

Prentoulis, M., Tumber, H., and Webster, F. (2005) 'Finding Space: Women Reporters at War', *Feminist Media Studies*, 5/3: 374–7.

Press Gazette (2012a) 'Press Gazette's Top Fifty Political Reporters', 27 Sept., retrieved Dec. 2012, from www.pressgazette.co.uk/press-gazettes-top-50-political-reporters.

Press Gazette (2012b) 'If You Ask Me: FT Weekend Editor Caroline Daniel', 18 Oct., retrieved Dec. 2012, from www.pressgazette.co.uk/if-you-ask-me-ft-weekend-editor-caroline-daniel.

Press Gazette (2012c) 'Martin Samuel Named Top UK Sports Journalist', 22 Oct., retrieved Dec. 2012, from www.pressgazette.co.uk/martin-samuel-named-top-uk-sports-journalist-press-gazette-top-50-poll.

Press Gazette (2012d) 'The British Journalism Awards 2012', 2 Nov., retrieved Dec. 2012, from www.pressgazette.co.uk/british-journalism-awards-2012-finalists-revealed.

Private Eye (2012) 'Street of Shame', 14 Dec., p. 6.

Reich, Z. (2013) 'Islands of Divergence in a Stream of Convergence', *Journalism Studies*, forthcoming.

Ricchiardi, S. (2001) 'Where Women Rule', *American Journalism Review* (Jan.-Feb.), retrieved July 2013, from www.ajr.org/Article.asp?id=803.

Rutter, J. (2012) 'Whitehall is in Danger of Reverting to White, Male Type', 14 Aug., retrieved Dec. 2012, from www.guardian.co.uk/commentisfree/2012/aug/14/whitehall-white-male-civil-service.

Rutter, J. (2013) 'Bridesmaids Revisited', 9 Jan., retrieved Jan. 2013, from www.instituteforgovernment.org.uk/blog/5313/bridesmaids-revisited.

Sabbagh, D. (2013) 'I've Been Allowed a Second Act', *Guardian*, 14 Jan., p. 31.

Sandberg, S. (2013) *Lean In: Women, Work and the Will to Lead* (London: W.H. Allen).

Sebba, A. (1994) *Battling for News: The Rise of the Woman Reporter* (London: Hodder & Stoughton).

Sieghart, M.-A., and Henry, G. (1998) *The Cheaper Sex: How Women Lose out in Journalism* (London: Women in Journalism).

Skillset (2010) *Women in the Creative Media Industries Report*, Sept., retrieved Dec. 2012, from www.creativeskillset.org/tv/freelancers/women/article_7851_1.asp.

Skillset (2012) *Television Sector – Labour Market Intelligence Profile*, retrieved July 2013, from www.creativeskillset.org/uploads/pdf/asset_16890.pdf.

Slier, P. (2013) 'Women in Warzones: An Added Risk?', 18 Mar., retrieved Apr. 2013, from http://themediaonline.co.za/2013/03/women-in-warzones-an-added-risk.

Sound Women on Air (2013) '1 in 5 Solo Voices is Female', retrieved July 2013, from www.soundwomen.co.uk/research.

Summerfield, P. (1984) *Women Workers in the Second World War* (London: Croom Helm).

Thompson, H. (2013) 'I'm Coming to Rape You Bitch: Is Online Abuse Silencing Female Journalists?', *XCity Magazine*, 27 (spring): 48–50.

Veeneman, A. (2013) 'Should There Be More Female Journalists at Westminster?', 11 Jan., retrieved Jan. 2013, from http://kettlemag.com/article/should-there-be-more-female-journalists-westminster.

Weaver, D., et al. (2007) *The American Journalist in the 21st Century* (Mahwah, NJ: Lawrence Erlbaum Associates).

WIJ (2007) 'The Lady Vanishes at 45', retrieved Dec. 2012, from http://womeninjournalism.co.uk/the-lady-vanishes-at-45.

WIJ (2012) 'Seen But Not Heard: How Women Make Front Page News', retrieved Jan. 2013, from http://womeninjournalism.co.uk/wp-content/uploads/2012/10/Seen_but_not_heard.pdf.

Williams, A. (2010) 'Post-Feminism at Work: The Experience of Female Journalists in the UK', University of Nottingham, PhD thesis.

Women's Media Center (2012) *The Status of Women in the US Media* (New York: Women's Media Center).

Wyatt, P. (2000) 'Pinching Men's Bottoms Can Be Bad for You', in S. Glover, *The Penguin Book of Journalism: The Secrets of the Press* (London: Penguin), 71–8.

Zelizer, B. (2005) 'The Culture of Journalism', in J. Curran and M. Gurevitch (eds), *Mass Media and Society* (London: Hodder Arnold).

Zoonen, L. van (1994) *Feminist Media Studies* (London: Sage).

Zoonen, L. van (1998) 'One of the Girls: The Changing Gender of Journalism', in C. Carter, G. Branston and S. Allan (eds), *News Gender and Power* (London: Routledge).

Acknowledgements

The research for this book involved a wide range of face to face interviews with women from across the spectrum of journalism; including print, broadcast, online, employed, freelancers and covering a range of positions and ages. Many of the interviewees are named and credited in the text but a number of others preferred to speak confidentially about their experiences and I am grateful to all of them for giving me their time and their insights. Very many thanks to Rebecca Suner, Sofie Harder, and Camilla Turner who were extremely helpful in compiling the research for this project – it would not have been possible without them. I hope their careers will in due course benefit from some of the insights raised in this work. Thanks also to Joanne Butcher and Lisa Nelson at the National Council for the Training of Journalists. Several of my colleagues, at City University and elsewhere, were also very helpful and in particular I would like to pay tribute to Daniel Franklin, Sarah Lonsdale, Steve Barnett, Jean Seaton, Charles Miller, Roy Greenslade, Mel Bunce, Barbara Schofield, Michael Bromley, Lis Howell, George Brock and Howard Tumber. Finally a big thanks to everyone at the RISJ, especially Robert Picard and Alex Reid and to the 2012 Reuters Fellows who participated in the discussions on this subject.